NAPA VALLEY

THE ULTIMATE WINERY GUIDE

Napa Valley

The Ultimate Winery Guide

Revised and Updated

❧

By Antonia Allegra

Photography by Richard Gillette

Foreword by Robert Mondavi

CHRONICLE BOOKS

San Francisco

Printed in China.

Library of Congress Cataloging-in-Publication Data:

Allegra, Antonia.
    Napa Valley : the ultimate winery guide / by Antonia Allegra ;
photography by Richard Gillette.—Rev. and updated.
       p.   cm.
    Includes index.
    ISBN 0-8118-1544-7 (pb)
     1. Wine and wine making—California—Napa Valley.   I. Gillette,
Richard. II. Title.
TP557.A55   1997   96-30636
641.2′2′0974919—dc20   CIP

Distributed in Canada by Raincoast Books
8680 Cambie Street, Vancouver, B.C. V6P 6M9

10 9 8 7 6 5 4 3 2 1

Editing: Carey Charlesworth and Steve Anderson
Book and cover design: Lisa Levin

Chronicle Books
85 Second Street
San Francisco, CA 94105

Web Site: www.chronbooks.com

ACKNOWLEDGMENTS

&

We extend special thanks to these people who

went out of their way to help us create this book:

Maynard Amerine, Michael Carabetta,

Martha Casselman, Carey Charlesworth, Sue Farley,

Mary Frances Fisher, Jim Frisinger, Kelly Johnson,

Leslie Jonath, Natalie Joyce, Bill LeBlond,

Lisa Levin, Malinda Pryde, Ellen Russell, Bill Ryan,

Bob Steinhauer, John and Gladys Wichels and,

especially, Harvey Posert.

CONTENTS

Foreword   10

An Invitation

Introduction   14

Overview

Map   20

The Operations of a Vineyard Year   21

Winery Tours

Wineries by Napa Valley Region   24

Wineries by Town   24

Ideal Visiting Seasons for Wineries   24

Wineries Recommended for

Your Special Interests   24

Triangle Tours   26

The Wineries

Beaulieu Vineyards   30

Beringer Vineyards   32

Cakebread Cellars   34

Chateau Montelena   36

Chimney Rock Winery   38

Clos du Val   40

Clos Pegase   42

Codorniu Napa   44

Cuvaison Winery   48

Domaine Carneros   50

Domaine Chandon   54

Flora Springs Winery   56

Freemark Abbey Winery   60

Grgich Hills Cellars   62

The Hess Collection Winery   64

Charles Krug Winery   68

Louis M. Martini Winery   70

Robert Mondavi Winery   72

Mumm Napa Valley   76

Niebaum-Coppola Estate Winery   78

Joseph Phelps Vineyards   82

Rutherford Hill Winery   86

St. Clement Vineyards   88

St. Supéry Vineyards & Winery   90

Schramsberg Vineyards   92

Stag's Leap Wine Cellars   94

Sterling Vineyards   96

Sutter Home Winery   98

Trefethen Vineyards   100

V. Sattui Winery   102

Resources

Chambers of Commerce   106

Educational Sources   106

Libraries   106

Museums   106

Newspapers   106

Magazines   106

Touring and Wine Making

On Touring Wineries   110

On Wine and Wine Making   110

On Barrels   111

Directory

A Directory of Napa Valley Wineries   114

Index   118

FOREWORD

Welcome to our lovely Napa Valley and to all its wineries! Whether you journey on Highway 29 or the Silverado Trail or take the armchair route through the pages of this book, you'll find numerous older wineries and many new ones eager to show you our renowned hospitality. Through the winery tours and your visits in our towns and restaurants, your enjoyment of wine will grow as you learn more about this land and its wonderful people. ❧ Each winery has its own point of view about grape growing and wine making—that's what makes wine so interesting. As you visit the individual wineries, ask about special programs on wine making, on the arts, and on wine and food. We all want to play a part in forming your happy memories of this valley. Bringing wine together with the arts and culture has been a special focus of my career. Even though ours is one of the newer wineries—it was the first winery built after Prohibition, in 1966—we join in a long tradition of wine and gastronomy as well as the fine arts: music, painting, sculpture, theater, and writing, and, here especially, architecture. ❧ Wine is the natural beverage for every celebration: the birth of a child, graduation, engagements, weddings, anniversaries, promotions, family gatherings, toasts between governments, and many other occasions. Wine can stand the scrutiny of any responsible citizen, because its benefits have been recognized for more than seven thousand years . . . since civilization began. And common sense tells us that wine will be with us forever as an integral part of our culture, heritage, and gracious way of life. ❧ I always knew that Napa Valley had the soils, climate, grape varieties, and people to make wines that rank on a par with the finest wines of the world. Fortunately, we have in the past decade been able to show connoisseurs in the Old and New Worlds that this is so; and we hope that you will share our enthusiasm, success, and enjoyment.

I raise a glass to the many guests who will enjoy this book and to their visits in the Napa Valley. "To your health!"

Robert Mondavi

INTRODUCTION

The play of color against the thirty-mile symmetry of neat vineyards bonds visitors and residents to this Napa Valley. ∾ As you drive along the two north-south thoroughfares, the gentle mountain ranges act as backdrop to spectacular views, dappled with vineyard colors that depend on the time of year—the bright yellow of mustard plants at the feet of dormant vines in spring; a rich, verdant carpet of summer's grape leaves; the autumn olive, rust, burgundy, and sienna of a Renaissance tapestry; and finally the somber black and brown tones of winter. Sometimes, seen from an auto at fifty miles per hour, trellis wires give the impression of sheets of silver. The quality of light in this region is often extraordinary and has been the inspiration for many an artist's eye. ∾ If your eye grabs a point and moves with it, you will see a blur of color. But allow the view to skip from row to row of vines and it will seem to be a series of mirrors, channels reflecting plants in various stages of life. In fact, it is the constant awareness of the life-growth-harvest cycle of renewal that invokes reflectiveness throughout the year. ∾ The Napa Valley has been an agricultural hub since well before the Civil War. This was originally home to the Wappo and other tribes of Native Americans. Then, under General Mariano Vallejo, the area became Mexican California until the Bear Flag Republic revolt. In those early years, wheat, apples, prunes, walnuts, and a few grape vines were planted in the rocky soil. With the Victorian boom and the rise in popularity of locally made wines, the region flourished socially as well as agriculturally. The Prohibition years (1919–1933) closed most wineries and halted local development, but the valley has thrived since the mid-1960s and is again a popular visitors' spot. It was recently named the third most popular natural tourist attraction in the state of California, following San Francisco and Yosemite. ∾ Napa, Yountville, Oakville, Rutherford, St. Helena, and Calistoga dot the thirty-mile-long, five-mile-wide string of towns and cities along Highway 29 and the Silverado Trail. They act as centers for the locals and lodging, dining, and shopping places for visitors. But most of the valley's activity happens in the fields. ☙ Ninety percent of this valley is dedicated to agricultural use, and unlike neighboring Sonoma County, most of the earth on this side of the Mayacamas Range is planted to vines. Hillsides or meadows of cattle, horses, sheep, or goats are rare here. At twenty thousand to forty thousand dollars an acre, the land is too expensive for any cultivation other than grapes. As a result, this is an American wine-lover's paradise. ☙ Those who have visited the wine regions of Europe will see similarities in the rocky grape-growing terrains and occasionally in the vistas. However, I believe that there is one major difference from the tourist's point of view: in Europe, a vineyard visit is just that, a walk in the vineyard, if you're lucky. More often, it is a descent into a cool basement to taste some wine and make a purchase. If you wish to see imposing architecture accessible to the public, you must travel to the various chateaux regions that often are near but separated from the vineyards. And they often require special reservations. ☙ Here in the Napa Valley, a visitor has the best of all worlds. Superb wines are available at any of more than two hundred wineries, and often the establishments are housed in magnificent structures themselves worthy of castle-visits. As it turns out, winery owners are the royalty of the Napa Valley, their kingdoms being vineyards and wineries. ☙ Perhaps this valley is so loved because it offers a magical sense of familiarity. For instance, this could easily be the setting for Jack in the Beanstalk's Happy Valley of fairy-tale lore. And millions viewed these hills and vineyards weekly during the screening of the "Falcon Crest" television series. But even more, being here feels like a homecoming to the best of rural America's simple life. ☙ In my hometown of St. Helena, certain daily observations still strike me as gifts rather than facts of life. I have lived in big cities and nothing there offers such basic pleasure as the morning greeting from the postman when I pick up my mail or the sound of frogs croaking on starry spring nights. The OK Barber Shop on Main Street hasn't changed its interior in at least fifty years, and its dull green, ecru, and chrome fixtures aren't likely to switch to those of a styling salon. Crusty country loaves continue to exit hot from the Model Bakery's brick oven, and the town merchants chatter in the morning light as they sweep their sidewalk footage. Crime decreased by 31 percent in 1989 in St. Helena; there wasn't much to speak of before that. And a call-to-alarm alerts volunteer Fire Department members and townspeople of some strain in the otherwise calm life of the town. ✂ There are other images, too. There's a freckled boy—maybe ten years old—who frequently bicycles to school, tugging his laughing pal on a skateboard tied to the end of a rope. There is a sweet down-home honesty about this place. ✂ Ever-present birds add their joyful touch to daily life. Occasionally a flock of red-winged blackbirds will swoop to a fence rail, exposing a sudden surprise of brilliant red feathers at their shoulders. Or, when unpicked grapes still hang like udders from vines in December, it's not unusual for the sky to be filled with careening, twittering starlings, drunk from the yeasty vineyard fruit. ✂ Many Napa Valley residents grow grapes instead of lawn. With the drought of the 1980s and 1990s, a vineyard is more practical, requires no mowing, and yields wine grapes, which can be sold or pressed into wine. In fact, the residents can "drink their lawn." ✂ Where else in America would you see a "No Winery This Lane" sign along the highway? Or find almost three pages of winery listings in the telephone book? ✂ Often, with more than two hundred wineries on a valley list, it can be difficult to choose which to visit. And friends have told me, "We can't go wrong tasting Napa Valley wines, but we want to visit Victorian homes, too." To guide their preferences, I developed a personal annotated list for family and friends. Wineries with art collections. Spectacular gardens. Technical tours. Once on a serious path, I toured and screened wineries in the valley that are open to visitors. The wineries had to offer tours and be easily accessible, interesting, and visitor-friendly. To write this book,

I finally identified the thirty wineries that I believe fascinate and entertain visitors most with the Napa Valley wine making art and way of life. My list is by no means meant to limit you in your travels in the Napa Valley. All the wineries here are marvelous, each with a different story and beauty. ❧ In all cases, I took standard tours. I did not seek or accept any gifts. The wineries chosen are here because they go out of their way to make visiting an educational and sensual pleasure. These are the wineries I suggest to my friends. ❧ I do not wish to overlook the multiple ways to view the Napa Valley. By air, there are hot air balloons, gliders, and biplanes. You can travel by bicycle or by train or you can hike. And the possibilities for outstanding meals here are legendary. ❧ No matter how you visit here, no matter whether you stay at a resort, a hotel, a bed and breakfast inn, or in your friend's guest room, expect daily brushes with beauty mixed with the reality of the vineyard year. The combination may take you unawares. Though this splendid valley of vines and winery "castles" may seem small, its greatness will be evident—in its people and in its wines.

Antonia Allegra
St. Helena, California

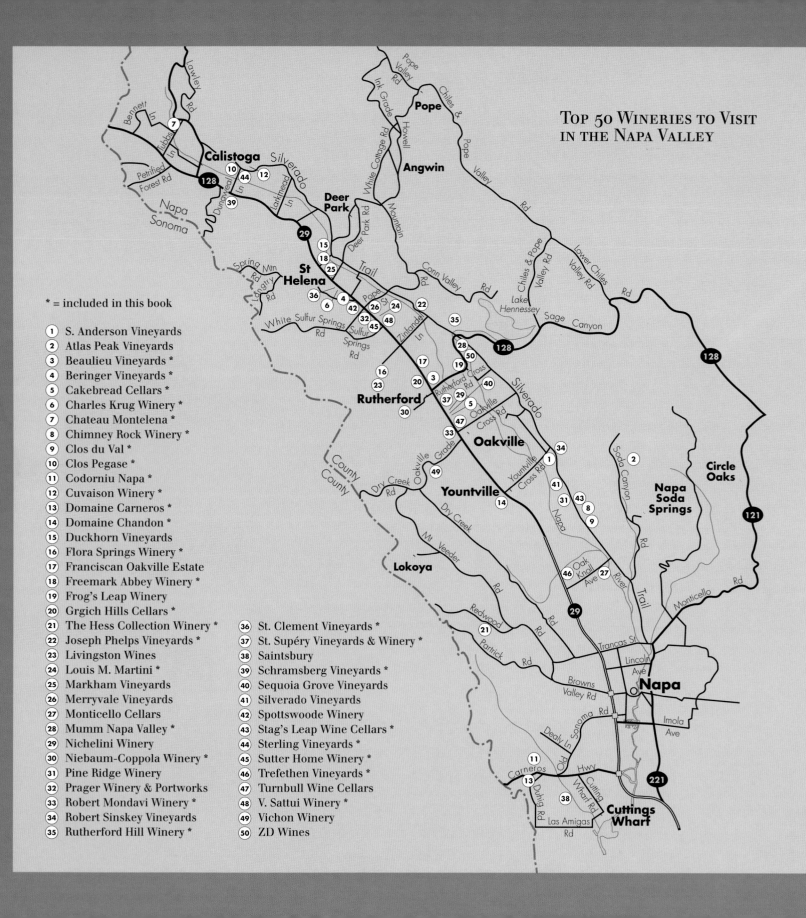

Top 50 Wineries to Visit in the Napa Valley

* = included in this book

1. S. Anderson Vineyards
2. Atlas Peak Vineyards
3. Beaulieu Vineyards *
4. Beringer Vineyards *
5. Cakebread Cellars *
6. Charles Krug Winery *
7. Chateau Montelena *
8. Chimney Rock Winery *
9. Clos du Val *
10. Clos Pegase *
11. Codorniu Napa *
12. Cuvaison Winery *
13. Domaine Carneros *
14. Domaine Chandon *
15. Duckhorn Vineyards
16. Flora Springs Winery *
17. Franciscan Oakville Estate
18. Freemark Abbey Winery *
19. Frog's Leap Winery
20. Grgich Hills Cellars *
21. The Hess Collection Winery *
22. Joseph Phelps Vineyards *
23. Livingston Wines
24. Louis M. Martini *
25. Markham Vineyards
26. Merryvale Vineyards
27. Monticello Cellars
28. Mumm Napa Valley *
29. Nichelini Winery
30. Niebaum-Coppola Winery *
31. Pine Ridge Winery
32. Prager Winery & Portworks
33. Robert Mondavi Winery *
34. Robert Sinskey Vineyards
35. Rutherford Hill Winery *

36. St. Clement Vineyards *
37. St. Supéry Vineyards & Winery *
38. Saintsbury
39. Schramsberg Vineyards *
40. Sequoia Grove Vineyards
41. Silverado Vineyards
42. Spottswoode Winery
43. Stag's Leap Wine Cellars *
44. Sterling Vineyards *
45. Sutter Home Winery *
46. Trefethen Vineyards *
47. Turnbull Wine Cellars *
48. V. Sattui Winery *
49. Vichon Winery
50. ZD Wines

control, suckering (removing undesirable shoots), sulfuring (to prevent mildew), fertilizing, vine tying/vine training

December: Major machinery maintenance, weed spraying, ongoing installation of irrigation and frost control systems, vineyard development operations, soil preparation

January: Weeding, spraying, pruning, vine tying/vine training, major machinery maintenance

May: Irrigation, foliar spraying on leaves, planting, suckering, cultivating/discing, frost control, fertilizing, vine tying/vine training, sulfuring

September: Harvesting, grafting, berry sampling, ongoing installation of irrigation and frost control systems, vineyard development operations, soil preparation

February: Pruning, vine tying/vine training, major machinery maintenance, rootstock pulled from nursery/stored, budwood selection/storage

October: Harvesting, ongoing installation of irrigation and frost control systems, vineyard development operations, soil preparation

March: Vine tying/vine training, cultivating, discing, frost control

June: Foliar spraying on leaves, cultivating/discing, suckering, grafting, irrigation, frost control, crop thinning, fertilizing, vine tying/vine training, sulfuring

July: Cultivating/discing, irrigation vine tying/vine training, berry (actual description of and industry name for grape) sampling

April: Planting rootstock and benchgrafts, cultivating/ discing, foliar spraying-fertilization, irrigation, frost

August: Irrigation, hedging, harvesting, grafting, berry sampling, ongoing installation of irrigation and frost control systems, vineyard development operations, soil preparation

November: Major machinery maintenance, weed spraying, chiseling (breaking up soil compaction), ongoing installation of irrigation and frost control systems, vineyard development operations, soil preparation

WINERY TOURS

WINERIES BY NAPA VALLEY REGION

DOWN-VALLEY (SOUTH)
Chimney Rock Winery

Clos Du Val

Codorniu Napa

Domaine Carneros

Domaine Chandon

The Hess Collection Winery

Stag's Leap Wine Cellars

Trefethen Vineyards

MID-VALLEY (CENTRAL)
Beaulieu Vineyards

Cakebread Cellars

Grgich Hills Cellars

Robert Mondavi Winery

Mumm Napa Valley

Niebaum-Coppola Estate
    Winery

Rutherford Hill Winery

St. Supéry Vineyards & Winery

UP-VALLEY (NORTH)
Beringer Vineyards

Chateau Montelena

Clos Pegase

Cuvaison Winery

Freemark Abbey Winery

Charles Krug Winery

Louis M. Martini Winery

Joseph Phelps Vineyards

St. Clement Vineyards

Schramsberg Vineyards

Sterling Vineyards

Sutter Home Winery

V. Sattui Winery

WINERIES BY TOWN

CALISTOGA
Chateau Montelena

Clos Pegase

Cuvaison Winery

Schramsberg Vineyards

Sterling Vineyards

NAPA
Chimney Rock Winery

Clos du Val

Codorniu Napa

Domaine Carneros

The Hess Collection Winery

Stag's Leap Wine Cellars

Trefethen Vineyards

OAKVILLE
Robert Mondavi Winery

RUTHERFORD
Beaulieu Vineyards

Cakebread Cellars

Grgich Hills Cellars

Mumm Napa Valley

Niebaum-Coppola Estate
    Winery

Rutherford Hill Winery

St. Supéry Vineyards & Winery

ST. HELENA
Beringer Vineyards

Flora Springs Winery

Freemark Abbey Winery

Charles Krug Winery

Louis M. Martini Winery

Joseph Phelps Vineyards

St. Clement Vineyards

Sutter Home Winery

V. Sattui Winery

YOUNTVILLE
Domaine Chandon

IDEAL VISITING SEASONS FOR WINERIES

WINTER
Chimney Rock Winery

Domaine Carneros

Freemark Abbey Winery

The Hess Collection Winery

SPRING
Beringer Vineyards

Codorniu Napa

Domaine Chandon

Charles Krug Winery

Niebaum-Coppola Estate
    Winery

Joseph Phelps Vineyards

Sterling Vineyards

SUMMER
Chateau Montelena

Clos Pegase

Cuvaison Winery

Grgich Hills Cellars

Louis M. Martini Winery

Rutherford Hill Winery

Schramsberg Vineyards

Stag's Leap Wine Cellars

Sutter Home Winery

V. Sattui Winery

AUTUMN
Beaulieu Vineyards

Cakebread Cellars

Clos Du Val

Robert Mondavi Winery

Mumm Napa Valley

St. Clement Vineyards

St. Supéry Vineyards & Winery

Trefethen Vineyards

WINERIES RECOMMENDED FOR YOUR SPECIAL INTERESTS

ATTENTION TO WINE WITH FOOD
Beringer Vineyards

Cakebread Cellars

Domaine Carneros

Domaine Chandon

Grgich Hills Cellars

Robert Mondavi Winery

Mumm Napa Valley

Niebaum-Coppola Estate
    Winery

Rutherford Hill Winery

St. Supéry Vineyards & Winery

Stag's Leap Wine Cellars

Sterling Vineyards

V. Sattui Winery

CAVES

Beringer Vineyards

Clos Pegase

Rutherford Hill Winery

St. Clement Vineyards

Schramsberg Vineyards

CHAMPAGNE/ SPARKLING WINE

Beaulieu Vineyards

Codorniu Napa

Domaine Carneros

Domaine Chandon

Robert Mondavi Winery

Mumm Napa Valley

Schramsberg Vineyards

CONTEMPORARY ART COLLECTIONS

Clos Pegase

Codorniu Napa

The Hess Collection Winery

Robert Mondavi Winery

St. Supéry Vineyards & Winery

CONTEMPORARY OR SPECIAL ARCHITECTURE

Cakebread Cellars

Chimney Rock Winery

Clos Pegase

Codorniu Napa

The Hess Collection Winery

Robert Mondavi Winery

Joseph Phelps Vineyards

Rutherford Hill Winery

Sterling Vineyards

FRENCH CHATEAU-STYLE ARCHITECTURE

Chateau Montelena

Domaine Carneros

GARDENS

Beringer Vineyards

Cakebread Cellars

Chateau Montelena

Chimney Rock Winery

Domaine Chandon

Freemark Abbey Winery

Louis M. Martini Winery

Robert Mondavi Winery

Niebaum-Coppola Estate
Winery

Joseph Phelps Vineyards

St. Clement Vineyards

Schramsberg Vineyards

Stag's Leap Wine Cellars

Sutter Home Winery

Trefethen Vineyards

V. Sattui Winery

OUTSTANDING PANORAMAS

Chateau Montelena

Chimney Rock Winery

Codorniu Napa

Domaine Carneros

Charles Krug Winery

Niebaum-Coppola Estate
Winery

Joseph Phelps Vineyards

Rutherford Hill Winery

Sterling Vineyards

OUTSTANDING TOURS

Domaine Chandon

Robert Mondavi Winery

Mumm Napa Valley

St. Supéry Vineyards & Winery

PICNIC SETTINGS

Beaulieu Vineyards

Clos Pegase

Cuvaison Winery

Freemark Abbey Winery

Louis M. Martini Winery

Joseph Phelps Vineyards

Rutherford Hill Winery

Stag's Leap Wine Cellars

V. Sattui Winery

SELF-TOURS

The Hess Collection Winery

St. Supéry Vineyards & Winery

Sterling Vineyards

Sutter Home Winery

V. Sattui Winery

STAINED GLASS WINDOWS

Beringer Vineyards

St. Clement Vineyards

Sterling Vineyards

VICTORIAN HOMES, INTERIORS

Beringer Vineyards

St. Clement Vineyards

St. Supéry Vineyards & Winery

Sutter Home Winery

VINEYARD VISITS

Cakebread Cellars

Chimney Rock Winery

Clos du Val

Grgich Hills Cellars

Charles Krug Winery

Robert Mondavi Winery

St. Supéry Vineyards & Winery

Trefethen Vineyards

WINE-MAKING EMPHASIS

Cakebread Cellars

Clos du Val

Cuvaison Winery

Domaine Carneros

Domaine Chandon

Grgich Hills Cellars

Charles Krug Winery

Louis M. Martini Winery

Robert Mondavi Winery

Mumm Napa Valley

St. Supéry Vineyards & Winery

Schramsberg Vineyards

Stag's Leap Wine Cellars

Trefethen Vineyards

TRIANGLE TOURS

Three winery tours per day—or fewer—is an ideal scheduling goal for an enjoyable stay in the Napa Valley. This takes into consideration a first tour starting around 10 A.M. and time for lunch at one of the many fine restaurants here or out of your own picnic hamper. Plan time to visit the towns, as well, which offer museums, shopping, and historical attractions that should not be overlooked. Wineries close by 5:30 P.M. at the latest, allowing time to rest before the evening meal.

Below you'll find examples of day-trip winery destinations in geographically balanced "triangles." They're starting points for your imagination. These triangle tours do not take into account specific interests, such as a fascination with Victorian architecture, or a passion for contemporary art, or a yearning to visit gardens. (See recommendations according to these and other interests on p. 24.) Nor do they list specific restaurants in the various regions. For restaurant listings, check with the various Chambers of Commerce or turn to locals for friendly suggestions. I've suggested picnicking when one or more wineries in the suggested triangle offers a comfortable picnic setting.

Remember that the valley's thirty-mile length means at least one hour of driving for a round trip from either end, from Napa or Calistoga. This shortens the time for touring. You might consider midvalley accommodations or lodging at one end of the valley one night and the opposite the next. Or zigzag through the valley, cutting through the vineyards on one of the lateral roads off Highway 29 or the Silverado Trail. Bear in mind that, even at its broadest point, the valley is only five miles wide.

Whatever your plans, relax and enjoy every minute of your stay.

FROM DOWN-VALLEY (SOUTH)

- The Hess Collection Winery/lunch in Napa/Trefethen Vineyards/Domaine Chandon
- Clos du Val/Chimney Rock Winery/picnic at Stag's Leap Cellars/Stag's Leap Wine Cellars
- Codorniu Napa/Domaine Carneros/late lunch in Napa or Carneros region/The Hess Collection Winery

FROM MID-VALLEY (CENTRAL)

- Robert Mondavi Winery/lunch in Oakville/Cakebread Cellars/Niebaum-Coppola Estate Winery
- St. Supéry Vineyards & Winery/picnic at Rutherford Hill Winery/Rutherford Hill Winery/Mumm Napa Valley
- Niebaum-Coppola Estate Winery/lunch in Oakville or Rutherford or picnic at Beaulieu Vineyards/Beaulieu Vineyards/Grgich Hills Cellars

FROM UP-VALLEY (NORTH)

- Freemark Abbey Winery/lunch in St. Helena/Charles Krug Winery/Beringer Vineyards
- Cuvaison Winery/picnic at Cuvaison Winery or Clos Pegase/Clos Pegase/Sterling Vineyards
- Joseph Phelps Vineyards/picnic at Joseph Phelps or at Louis M. Martini Winery/Louis M. Martini Winery/Sutter Home Winery
- St. Clement Vineyards/lunch in St. Helena or in Calistoga/Schramsberg Vineyards/Sterling Vineyards
- Spring Mountain Winery/picnic at V. Sattui Winery/V. Sattui Winery/Sutter Home Winery
- Chateau Montelena/Cuvaison Winery/lunch in Calistoga or picnic at Cuvaison or Clos Pegase/Clos Pegase

Beaulieu Vineyards
1960 St. Helena Highway
Rutherford, CA 94573
(707) 963-2411;
telefax (707) 963-5920

Winemaker: Joel Aiken
Winery owner: Heublein, Inc.

Access
Location: On the corner of Rutherford Road (Highway 128) and Highway 29.

Hours open for visits and tastings: Weekdays 10 A.M.–5 P.M., weekends 10 A.M.–5 P.M., except New Year's Day, Easter, Thanksgiving, and Christmas. Tours given continuously.

Appointment necessary for tour? No.

Wheelchairs accommodated? Yes.

Tastings
Charge for tasting with tour? No.

Charge for tasting without tour? No, except for select older vintages.

Typical wines offered: Sauvignon Blanc, Chardonnay, Cabernet Sauvignon.

Sales of wine-related items? Yes, including logo glasses.

Picnics and Programs
Picnic area open to the public? No.

Special events or wine-related programs? Beaulieu Wine Society (no charge for membership). Members receive 2 bottles of wine each month at discount; discounts at winery and by mail, VIP tour and tasting at winery, with advance reservation; and invitations to various special events.

Sensory evaluations offered periodically following tours.

You can learn a tremendous amount about wine making at Beaulieu Vineyards even before the tour begins. On entering the barrel-shaped upper level of the visitors' center of this venerable winery, do be sure to walk the entire perimeter of the area. There are displays of wine-related implements, such as a collection of corkscrews, varying in style from modest to frivolous and dating back to 1900. Other entry-room presentations include one on coopering techniques, most procedures for which have not changed over centuries of barrel making. There is also an excellent corkwood exhibit that demonstrates a cork's passage from tree bark to newly cut, unfinished cork to the finished product: cleaned, champhered (edged), branded, and paraffined.

The tour guide leads across the shaded parking area to the crush pad behind the winery, which was greatly enlarged in 1969 when members of the original Georges de Latour family sold Beaulieu to Heublein, Inc. During crush, you're at wine maker level watching grapes rain into the steel crush pads, which resemble huge metal V-shaped troughs. Perhaps because of the friendliness between the guides and the winery workers, there is very little sense of a huge corporation here. Although there are relatively few cellarworkers year-round, 400 to 450 pickers are needed at harvest time and production yields 400,000 to 450,000 cases per year.

Next on the tour agenda, the group, which can vary in size from five to about twenty-five, is led to the "Valley of the Redwoods"—the area of the winery where eighty-five-year-old redwood tanks create a wooden alley aromatic with the Carneros Pinot Noir fermenting there.

Be sure to note the glass tubing running along the cement walls. With this system, fermented grape juice is pumped in a visible manner from one part of the winery to another, banding the cement stone walls with deep red or pale green, depending on the juices. You'll hear the bottling line activity in the background.

André Tchelistcheff, the revered active winemaker for the winery from 1928 until 1973, now acts in a consulting role, still contributing to the success of the Beaulieu wines. It was he who created the distinguishing hallmark of BV wines by putting the American grape juice in American oak or redwood, rather than in French oak barrels. Occasionally,

visitors will spot Tchelistcheff on his rounds with winemaker Joel Aiken.

The actual winery faces Highway 29, with a wall of ivy and Virginia Creeper covering the original brick and concrete building. It dates from 1885 and was owned by Seneca Ewer, one of the prominent landowners who joined the first circle of Napa Valley winemakers. Ewer's sale of the winery to Frenchman Georges de Latour was a fortuitous move for the history of wine making in the Napa Valley, as de Latour was an extremely zealous entrepreneur who extended word of his winery (named *beau lieu*; French for "beautiful place") through San Francisco social circles, making the wine a turn-of-the-century favorite.

The tour ends back at the visitors' center with a generous tasting of Beaulieu still and sparkling wines and the option of tasting older wines in the private tasting area. There, one-ounce pours of such vintages as '73, '81, '83, and '86 are sold for a nominal fee—a bargain, considering that these wines would normally sell for $37 to $70 per bottle.

BERINGER VINEYARDS

Beringer Vineyards

2000 Main Street
St. Helena, CA 94574
(707) 963-7115;
telefax (707) 963-1735

Winemaker: Ed Sbragia

Winery owners: Texas Pacific Group
& Silverado Partners

Access

Location: In the northern outskirts
of St. Helena on Highway 29 at the
"tunnel of trees."

Hours open for visits and tastings:
9:30 A.M.–5 p.m. May 1 through
October 30; 9:30 A.M.–4 P.M.
November 1 through April 30,
except New Year's Day, Easter, and
Christmas. Tours given continuously.

Appointment necessary for tour?
No. In summer, avoid crowds by
coming early in the day.

Wheelchairs accommodated? Yes.

Tastings

Charge for tasting with tour? No.

Charge for tasting without tour?
Yes, for reserve wines poured in the
Founders' Room ($2–$3 per glass),
not deductible from the price of
purchased wine.

Typical wines offered: Cabernet,
Napa Valley Chardonnay, Knight's
Valley Cabernet, White Meritage,
Red Meritage.

Sales of wine-related items?
Yes, including logo glasses ($5.50).

Picnics and Programs

Picnic area open to the public? No.

Special events or wine-related
programs? The School for American
Chefs, open to scholarship-winning
chefs only.

At Beringer, you can visit an elegant Victorian home, photograph seasonal flower beds, or explore century-old caves for wine aging. This winery has generated vintages since 1879, earning it the title of Napa Valley's oldest winery with continuous production. Even during Prohibition, the Beringer family was granted approval to produce sacramental and medicinal wines and brandies when other companies closed their doors. Because of its lengthy history and recognition, hundreds of thousands of tourists have journeyed to the valley with Beringer as their specific goal.

On turning onto the estate grounds, you will first see the impressive seventeen-room Rhine House, built in the 1880s. The Beringer brothers—businessman Frederick and winemaker Jacob—built the home to resemble their birthplace in Mainz, Germany. The slate roof, European stained glass windows, and inlaid wooden floors are all original, as is most

of the home, which was restored after 1971 when the winery was purchased by Nestlé, Inc., and then, in 1995, by a private partnership.

The walk south from the parking lot will lead you past the Hudson House, Jacob's home, where he, his wife, and their six children lived. It now houses Beringer's School for American Chefs, a program that brings some of the country's top professional chefs to the winery for scholarship studies with renowned culinary teacher Madeleine Kamman. The studies emphasize food with wine.

Visitors usually find the spring-flowering wisteria, azaleas, oleanders, and roses on the Beringer grounds unforgettable. If photography is your hobby, be sure to have film for this visit.

Due to the popularity of this winery tour, delays are frequent. However, tours begin every half-hour in the tour center on the terrace. Below is Ruth Asawa's delightful bronze fountain that depicts the history of wine making.

Inside the center, you will sit on benches, joining thirty to fifty other tourists. There the tour guide will review the history of the Beringer family and the winery, pointing to such historical photos as one of Hollywood stars Charles Laughton and Carole Lombard celebrating the end of Prohibition in 1933 at Beringer.

While strolling up the gentle slope backing the center, you'll learn of the hundred Chinese laborers who were hired to chisel a thousand feet of tunnels from the Spring Mountain foothills just west of the Hudson House. On that site, Jacob oversaw the construction of a gravity-flow winery, 104 feet long by 40 feet wide. It was completed in 1876. Although Beringer now makes wine in a more modern facility directly across Highway 29, the renowned reserve Cabernet Sauvignons are aged in French oak barrels within Jacob's original caves. Don't miss the hand-carved German barrels near the cave entrances.

The tour meanders through the caves, which have been restructured for seismic purposes but still impart a sense of the original cellars. There is even a wine library, which houses vintages as old as 1937, dusty with time.

No vineyard is visited on the tour; however, you will see demonstration vines showing the growth of Chardonnay, Cabernet, Sauvignon Blanc, and Merlot grapes, all of which are important for production of the winery's varietal wines.

Down in the main gardens, the "Soaked Oak" holds forth in a prominent corner. Branches of the massive deciduous oak tree curl back on each other like a corkscrew. Some tour guides say that roots of the two-hundred-plus-year-old tree stretched under the caves and up into barrels of wine to cause the tree's contorted form.

The last stop on the Beringer tour is the former dining room in the Rhine House. There you will taste three wines—perhaps four if port is poured. Take time to study the stained glass windows in that room and throughout the house; Beringer holds the finest stained glass collection in the Napa Valley. Insurance coverage on the Rhine House alone is now $6 million, a far cry from the original $28,000 construction costs for the entire Germanic Victorian. The main rooms of the home are open for inspection, including an upper bedroom now dubbed the Founders' Room, where special reserve wines are poured.

Guides at Beringer are the only ones in the valley to toast visitors as they taste wine. "To your health!" or "Have a great time in the valley!" are frequent salutes, accompanied by clinking glasses. Guests are encouraged to drink wine at home, even with simple family fare or ethnic dishes. By the time you walk back to the parking area, you'll have a deeper understanding of Victorian times and how wine making related to life then as well as now.

CAKEBREAD CELLARS

Cakebread Cellars

8300 St. Helena Highway
Rutherford, CA 94573
(707) 963-5221;
telefax (707) 963-1067

Winemaker: Bruce Cakebread
Winery owners:
The Cakebread Family

Access
Location: On Highway 29, north slightly over ½ mile from Oakville (½ mile north of Robert Mondavi Winery); look for stone walls and colorful flower beds.

Hours open for visits and tastings: 10 A.M.–4 P.M. daily, except New Year's Day, Easter, Thanksgiving, and Christmas.

Appointment necessary for tour? Yes; call 24 hours in advance or early the same morning.

Wheelchairs accommodated? Yes.

Tastings
Charge for tasting with tour? No.

Charge for tasting without tour? No.

Typical wines offered: Current vintages of Sauvignon Blanc, Chardonnay, Zinfandel, Merlot, Pinot Noir, Cabernet Sauvignon; two reserve wines, Chardonnay, Rutherford Reserve Cabernet.

Sales of wine-related items? Logo glasses only ($3.50).

Picnics and Programs
Picnic area open to the public? No.

Special events or wine-related programs? Yes, call for calendar.

Among the myriad wineries along the road between Napa and Calistoga, Cakebread Cellars stands out in a colorful way. In any season of the year, look for masses of flowers in bloom on the east side of the road in Rutherford, just about halfway along the thirty-mile stretch.

The exuberance of the flowers is mirrored in the strong family spirit that greets all visitors. A joyful work ethic has been passed from winery founders Jack and Delores Cakebread to their children and on to the winery staff, and through them to winery visitors.

The winery tour starts in the vineyard. There the informative, low-key tour opens with talk of the importance of the right land to grow the best grapes. "At an average cost of forty thousand dollars an acre or more, Napa Valley floor land is the second most expensive farm soil in the United States," notes the tour guide, who is swift to mention that the most expensive farm land is in Riverside, California. He notes that grapes are second only to cotton in agricultural importance to the state of California, where 75 percent of the nation's wine grapes, 90 percent of its table grapes, and 100 percent of raisin grapes are grown. "But all the vineyards combined in the Napa Valley only grow 6 percent of those wine grapes; and the first cash crop of grapes doesn't mature until four to five years after the rootstock is planted," he says, putting a realistic note on the thousands of rows of vines stretching the width of the valley.

There are now more than 260 use permits and 210 bonded, licensed wineries in the Napa Valley, but when Jack Cakebread decided to plant grapes in 1972, his was winery license number 38. At the time, he and his wife bought land just north of Oakville from elderly friends named Sturdivant with the understanding that the friends could live out their days on the property. Then when the Cakebreads came on board, they created a true mom-and-pop operation, with mechanical know-how and a strong sense of design from Jack and culinary savvy with a nutritious slant from Delores. They frequently travel to promote their Cabernet Sauvignon, Sauvignon Blanc, and Chardonnay.

Although the winery has grown from its early stages to a seventy-two-acre property with production of sixty-five thousand cases a year, it retains the hands-on feeling and remains a family project. Son Bruce is now the Cakebread winemaker; Dennis works as business manager for the company; and third son Steven is a business consultant for the winery. Delores has developed a culinary program for visiting chefs and wine writers to encourage them to be aware of local produce and other Napa Valley food resources and how to pair them with wine. Also, she oversees the floral welcome at the winery's entrance.

"This is a working winery. Please stay together as we tour the production area," admonishes the tour guide as you join a group of ten visitors in the air-conditioned building. The labyrinthine winery buildings, designed by William Turnbull, present a contemporary redwood barn architecture that blends easily into the landscape. Engineering buffs are intrigued with the ultramodern equipment, which offers such practical systems as a drainage process that allows a simultaneous hosing of machines, vats, walls, and floor as well as an air flow program that reduces electrical costs.

In the storage room, instructions for how to read notations, the brand marks and pencil jottings, on a wine barrel are clearly explained. "Here," says the tour guide pointing to one end of a barrel, "is the barrel maker's name. This notes the source of the wood. Next, the year the barrel was bought, followed by the wine initials [C.S. for Cabernet Sauvignon, for example] and finally the vintage and any special comments, such as ML for malolactic fermentation."

The guide fields all questions, including how the winemaker balances the oak influences in flavoring the fermented grape juice. "Believe me," he says, "the last thing we want is wine with the flavor of Chateau 2 x 4! Too much wood can be a real negative for wines which are made to lay down a long while."

There is no pressure to return to the tasting room, though most do so readily. Most tourists have gone out of their way to visit Cakebread for specific reasons, such as to tour the source of a bottle of wine opened to celebrate their anniversary or at their favorite restaurant. One tourist said, "It's nice to find out that the Cakebreads are real people who like their wine and their work . . . and beautiful flowers."

CHATEAU MONTELENA

Chateau Montelena

1429 Tubbs Lane
Calistoga, CA 94515
(707) 942-5105;
telefax (707) 942-4221

Winemaker: James P. "Bo" Barrett
Winery owner: James L. Barrett,
Managing General Partner

Access

Location: 2 miles north of
Calistoga's flashing light, turn
northeast on Tubbs Lane (a right
turn, coming from Calistoga).

Hours open for visits and tastings:
10 A.M.–4 P.M. daily, except major
holidays and private events.
Tours at 11 A.M. and 2 P.M.

Appointment necessary for tour? Yes.

Wheelchairs accommodated? Yes,
except in unpaved parking lot.

Tastings

Charge for tasting with tour?
$5 for three wines; deductible
from purchase of over $20.

Charge for tasting without tour?
As above.

Typical wines offered: Chardonnay,
Cabernet Sauvignon, Johannisberg
Riesling; when available, Zinfandel.

Sales of wine-related items? Yes.

Picnics and Programs

Picnic area open to the public? Yes,
by reservation only (very limited).

Special events or wine-related
programs? Semi-annual Open
House: first weekend in March and
first weekend in September.

Special customers receive notification
of wines before release and are
invited to a private party during
the summer.

In the manner of the faithful geyser up the road from Chateau Montelena, a discrete, major spurt in the wine world brought this Napa Valley winery to prominence. That burst of energy came in June, 1976, when for the first time the wines of California overcame the grapes of Gaul. During a critical blind tasting judged in Paris by nine French oenophiles, California wines came out on top, with Chateau Montelena '73 as the champion Chardonnay.

The judges could not have been more amazed. What might have surprised them as well is that this winery is housed in a building of truly Gallic origins. Designed after the great chateaux of Bordeaux and built by a French architect, this was one of the small, thriving wineries of the turn of the century. Winery walls are three to twelve feet thick, made of imported and native cut stone. Senator Alfred Tubbs, originally a Bostonian, was the owner who chose the French design of what was then the sixth largest winery in the valley.

The recently remodeled tasting room that you'll see on arrival gives little hint of the splendid chateau beneath it. The visitors' room is located on an upper floor in the rear of the chateau, but appreciation of the tradition and architecture of this winery demands making the short walk downhill,

to properly view the ivy-covered stone facade of this elegant estate. There is a splendid vista point from man-made Jade Lake, which fronts the chateau. From there, you'll view the chateau, the willow-framed lake, and the quaint red lacquered bridge that spans the lake from shore to the pavilions on an island.

Beyond the lake lie acres of Chateau Montelena vineyards, the home of Jim Barrett—who dubs himself a "caretaker of the land" instead of its owner—and Mount St. Helena, rising two thousand feet in the background. Some say this is the Napa Valley dream view; it is definitely a photo opportunity to consider seriously. Wildlife aficionados will find ducks, swans, turtles, catfish, and a number of wild birds using the island as sanctuary. Considering the heady floral perfume that laces summer's hot, dry air, thoughts of Monet's garden at Giverny may jump to mind. Cascading old-fashioned roses vie with flora and fauna in the full spectrum of colors and bouquets. In fact, there is a similar, idyllic quality to time spent chez Monet and at this winery.

Along one of the lakeside paths there is a plaque proclaiming an ancient Chinese proverb: "Peace and tranquility to all who enter here." The aphorism was placed by former owners Yort and Jeanne Frank, who lived in the chateau after Prohibition had forced closure of the business. Now the chateau is used for winery purposes only. Present owner Barrett, whose son Bo is winemaker, offers the same four varietals today as in 1972: Cabernet Sauvignon, Zinfandel, Chardonnay, and Riesling. Barrett says his background as an attorney gave him the proper perspective on a life in the wine industry: "I spent eighteen years giving pain to people," he explains; "now I spend my life giving them pleasure."

Pleasure they do receive. During a posttour tasting, a visitor from Miami explained that she particularly enjoys the winery's Riesling, which is sold only in-house, because "it's not high in tannin that would make me want a drink after I've had a drink."

And what of the famous Chateau Montelena Chardonnay, made with grapes grown in alluvial, volcanic, and sedimentary soils? It is definitely the most popular wine tasted and purchased at the winery, even years after the touted Paris tasting.

For those carrying away wine during the summer's sometimes-blistering heat, the winery offers recommendations on

transporting it: "While our vineyards are enjoying the heat, your wine will not appreciate the drastic change in temperature from our cellar. The temperature inside an automobile can easily reach 110 degrees, literally cooking the wine in the bottle. A telltale sign that the wine has been overheated is a leaking bottle. This is caused by the contraction and expansion of the cork in response to the drastic change in temperature. Please take care to protect your purchase by providing some insulation against heat or by removing it from your car, as we cannot be responsible for wine after it has left the chateau."

Wine is not all that visitors take with them on departing the chateau. Tour guide Tony Prince notes, "Most people come like pilgrims to taste the Chardonnay, and when they get here, the beauty of the place adds to the whole experience and they leave refreshed."

Chimney Rock Winery

5350 Silverado Trail
Napa, CA 94558
(707) 257-2641;
telefax (707) 257-2036

Winemaker: Douglas Fletcher
Winery owners:
Sheldon and Stella Wilson

Access

Location: 5 miles north of Napa on the Silverado Trail, just north of the Chimney Rock golf course.

Hours open for visits and tastings: 10 A.M.–5 P.M. daily, except Thanksgiving and Christmas.

Appointment necessary for tour? Yes.

Wheelchairs accommodated? Yes, except on tour.

Tastings

Charge for tasting with tour? $3; includes logo glass or credit towards wine purchase.

Charge for tasting without tour? $3, as above.

Typical wines offered: Five wines, current and older vintages of Fumé Blanc, Chardonnay, Cabernet Sauvignon.

Sales of wine-related items? Yes, including polo shirts, wine accessories, etched bottles for special occasions.

Picnics and Programs

Picnic area open to the public? No.

Special events or wine-related programs? Yes.

The iron gates that open onto Chimney Rock's driveway point the way to one of Napa Valley's more splendid views. Your eye moves from the valley floor up to the eastern hillside, where trellised vineyards stretch along the undulating earth. With or without leaves, the rows of vines follow the various curves and openings in the land. The property seems to stretch forever.

To the right of the entry road, the winery and hospitality center welcome guests for tours. Even though reservations are suggested, visitors are welcome to join weekday tours of the seventeenth-century-style Cape Dutch buildings. An interesting twist on wine tasting is that you'll be offered a glass of the winery's Chardonnay before tour departure, with the suggestion to "Bring along your glass as we walk." This touch enhances the feeling that visitors are sauntering about a gracious home, although Chimney Rock owners Hack and Stella Wilson actually live on the crest of a hill behind the property.

The South African Huguenot style of the Cape Dutch property is unique in the Napa Valley. The graceful roofline curves are particularly visible from the road before early summer, because the poplars that line the estate act as leaf-less sentinels, giving a full view of the various buildings on the estate.

The tour starts at the hearth in the well-lit entry room. Antique fireplace tools decorate the white walls. Occasionally the tour will include a visit to the private tasting room where an imposing seventeenth-century highboy from South Africa dominates one white wall. That and the other blanched walls of the hospitality center contrast with the rich tones of antique wooden tables, light fixtures, and accent pieces adorning the space. The chalky walls are a refreshing change from the more typical use of unadorned wood in wineries built in the Napa Valley over the last thirty years.

The tour moves outside to a shaded area where sunken waterfalls divide part of the terra-cotta tile patio. From there you'll have a full view of the frieze mounted atop the winery's back wall. The subject of this nine-by-thirty-eight-foot work of art is Ganymede, cup bearer to the gods. The eighteenth-century German sculptor Anton Anreith created the original for the Groot Constantia winery at the Cape Colony of South Africa, where Anreith was employed by the Dutch East India Company. To duplicate the masterpiece for Chimney Rock, the Wilsons commissioned California sculptor Michael Casey, resident restoration artist for the state capitol in Sacramento. Imagine mounting the fiberglass-reinforced concrete duplication, which weighs five tons!

Moving to the vineyards and then to the winery, you'll soon realize that this is one of the valley's small wineries. With only nine full-time employees, chances are strong that you'll meet Doug Fletcher, the winemaker, and that you'll be able to speak with him about his wines, which are made strictly in the French manner. Chardonnay, Sauvignon Blanc, Cabernet Sauvignon, Merlot, and Cabernet Franc grapes are all used to create Bordeaux- and Burgundy-style wines.

During the tour, at least one of the wines still in the barrel is extracted with a "wine thief" (a long glass pipette) and offered to guests in the barrel room. If you feel misty while tasting the wine, the cause might be the winery's *faux cave*

system of creating constant humidity by spraying a fine fog over the thousand aging barrels, which will yield fifteen thousand cases of wine.

Back at the wine tasting bar, as reserve Cabernet Sauvignon and other vintages are served, the story is recounted of how friendship with wine expert Alexis Lichine led Hack Wilson—a former hotelier and soft drink and beer marketer—to his 1980 purchase of Chimney Rock Golf Course in the Stags Leap District. Nine holes of the golf course still remain, but the Wilsons and their son Doug had the other nine holes bulldozed (about seventy-five acres). They planted their vineyard estate there based on Lichine's dictate to "Look at all of the regions; but when you buy, buy in Napa Valley, for Napa is to California what Bordeaux is to France."

Some would say they scored a hole-in-one by doing so.

CLOS DU VAL

Clos du Val

5330 Silverado Trail
Napa, CA 94558
(707) 259-2200;
telefax (707) 252-6125

Winemaker: Bernard Portet
Winery owner: John Goelet

Access

Location: 5 miles north of Napa on
the east side of the Silverado Trail.

Hours open for visits and tastings:
10 A.M.–5 P.M. daily, except New
Year's Day, Easter, Thanksgiving,
and Christmas.

Appointment necessary for tour?
Yes; call a day or two in advance.

Wheelchairs accommodated? Yes.

Tastings

Charge for tasting with tour?
No, except for group tours.

Charge for tasting without tour?
$3 per person.

Typical wines offered: Cabernet
Sauvignon, Semillon, Chardonnay,
Pinot Noir, Zinfandel, Merlot.

Sales of wine-related items?
Yes, including logo glasses ($3),
T-shirts; also, Ronald Searle winery
cartoon posters.

Picnics and Programs

Picnic area open to the public? Yes.

Special events or wine-related
programs? New-release program
for residents of California; wine
made available to members before
release to general distributors
with discounts.

The massive doors to the Clos du Val tasting room open to a cool visitors' room, a welcome contrast to the hundred-degree heat of a Napa Valley summer day. This room touts a twenty-eight-foot ceiling and a feeling of space to match the size of the front door. Here you'll find a collection of vintages since 1972 and friendly people proud of their work.

It is from the cavernous tasting room that tours depart, directly to the vineyards. This is a winery seriously involved with the land and in explaining the annual struggle with the soil to produce top-quality grapes. Tours are usually small—two to eight people—and they cover all stages of viticulture and enology.

The view from the vineyards, the tourists' first stop, is exceptional: immediately before you are acres of vineyards; north is Stag's Leap Wine Cellars and to the northeast is Robert Mondavi's private home atop Wappo Hill.

"See those roses?" asked one Clos du Val tour guide, pointing to rosebushes laden with yellow blossoms. "There is a Bordeaux tradition that says if the roses bear many blossoms, there will be a strong harvest." This is one explanation for the roses seen frequently bordering vineyards. An alternate explanation is that the buds act like canaries in a coal mine; if the birds weaken, miners take heed and head for a safer area. In this case, if the roses droop or show signs of disease, the grower will inspect the soil or rootstock for disease. In either case, both rose stories have their roots in France, as does Bernard Portet, the winery's first winemaker. Portet is the son of the former *régisseur* of Chateau Lafite, and he instills his love of French oak by insisting on French Nevers oak barrels for aging wine. The Cabernets are kept in oak for five to six years.

The vineyard tour takes you right to the soil that was once a lava bed. If you want to walk between the vines, you will. This is not a dainty sandal tour, unless you don't mind shaking out a few pebbles. If the grapes are at an edible stage, be assured you'll taste some.

Moving from the vineyards, you'll learn of the Clos du Val lands dotting various regions of the Napa Valley: Stags Leap (where the winery is situated), State Lane, in Yountville, and the Carneros region all host rootstock for this Bordeaux-style

winery. Cabernet Sauvignon, Merlot, Zinfandel, Semillon, Cabernet Franc, Pinot Noir, and Chardonnay grapes are bases for the wines, which are sold under the Clos du Val label as well as under the Joli Val name.

"We're going into the Red Room" is a favorite phrase for leading to the area of the winery where red wines are made. If you're aware of the trend toward cold-stabilized wines during the stage just before bottling, you may be interested to view the frozen stabilization of Cabernets, which started at this winery in 1991, thus marking Clos du Val as one of the pioneers in cold stabilizing red wines.

Just in case all this discussion leaves you out in the cold, a few words from winemaker Portet about how cold stabilization works: "We drop the wine temperature to twenty-eight degrees and leave it there so tartrate crystals will precipitate out here in the winery and not in the bottle at home." You may have seen residue at the bottom of wine bottles—those

"flakes" are often tartrates. They're not harmful, but they are not attractive, and this is why many wineries follow the practice of filtration by freezing.

For an unusual diversion, watch the barrel cleaner in action. When needed, it is fixed on the floor in an alley between layers of barrels. A sprinkler is turned on inside the barrel, causing the barrel to spin by water pressure. This is a reminder of the frivolously entertaining mechanical water gardens outside of Salzburg, but on a practical level.

The tour guide offers an excellent explanation of how to "read" a barrel and, more importantly for the home consumer, how to read a wine label. The latter instruction takes place back at the wine tasting bar in the visitors' center. While there, you may hear a comparison with Taltarni Vineyards in Australia. That is due to the fact that the same owner holds both vineyards; Dominique Portet, Bernard's brother, is the winemaker in Australia.

While enjoying the various wines, don't miss the collection of droll cartoons lightening the subject of wine. These full-color, framed originals by Ronald Searle hang on a wall near the huge entry door. They were commissioned by John Goelet, the owner of Clos du Val. I have observed tourists, glass of wine in hand, reading the cartoon wall and laughing out loud, thus enjoying two of life's finest pleasures. Three, if you count visiting the Napa Valley.

Clos Pegase

1060 Dunaweal Lane
Calistoga, CA 94515
(707) 942-4981;
telefax (707) 942-4993
email: clospegase@aol.com

Winemaker: John Quinones
Winery owners: Jan and
Mitsuko Shrem

Access

Location: On Highway 29, 7 miles
north of St. Helena, turn northeast
at Dunaweal Lane. The winery is on
the left after .7 mile, across from
the entrance to Sterling Vineyards.

Hours open for visits and tastings:
10:30 A.M.–5 P.M. daily, except
New Year's Day, Thanksgiving,
Christmas Eve, and Christmas.

Appointment necessary for tour?
No. Guided tours at 11 A.M. and
2 P.M. daily. Self-guided tours of
outdoor sculpture garden.

Wheelchairs accommodated? Yes.

Tastings

Charge for tasting with tour? No.

Charge for tasting without tour?
$2.50

Typical wines offered: Chardonnay,
Cabernet, Merlot, "Hommage"
Reserve Cabernet Sauvignon.

Sales of wine-related items? Yes.

Picnics and Programs

Picnic area open to the public?
Yes, on lawn under trees.

Special events or wine-related
programs? Wine club. The third
Saturday of each month, a free
slide presentation by Jan Shrem
based on 4,000 years of wine in
art. 11 A.M. to noon. The "Grapes
of Laugh" comedy competition
third Saturday of April, 5:30 P.M.
(reservations required).

Clos Pegase is a haven for lovers of art and antiquities. A visit to the winery demonstrates the lengths to which owners Jan and Mitsuko Shrem have gone to create a showplace for their Cabernets, Chardonnays, and other wines.

Before zeroing in on the final design of their winery, the owners initiated a national architectural design competition sponsored by the San Francisco Museum of Modern Art. The winery opened in 1987. Since then, Clos Pegase has garnered numerous international awards for Princeton architect Michael Graves. His winning design, a Greco-Roman temple to wine and the arts, makes an impressive statement from the moment you drive onto the estate.

Contemporary sculpture in the parking lot says it all: art reigns here. In fact, for frequent Clos Pegase visitors the tour guide will point out the latest additions to the collection, such as Jacques Lipschitz's *Bellerophon Taming Pegasus*, or Cesare Peverelli's *The Urban Gent*, or the giant bronze thumb by Cesar that rises out of the vineyards abutting the winery property.

Guests are welcome to sit on the grounds to picnic, according to Jan Shrem. "I want people to feel the connection between wine, food, and the arts," he says with a sweeping gesture of his hand.

Various public rooms at the winery run the gamut from the Harvest Room, thus named due to giant enlargements of vineyard scenes from the medieval *Book of Days* that adorn the walls, to well-lit caves lined with ancient Bacchanalian statuary. It is in one of the caves that Shrem offers the public a monthly slide show of wine as it has been depicted in art over the years.

While strolling from the tasting room through the winery caves and back again, tourists can't miss informative boards with key wine-in-art works related to wine in portraiture; wine in mythology; wine and religion; wine as a love potion; wine and the still life; and wine vessels, from the ancient to the contemporary. Surely if there be any questions as to the historical tradition of wine in society, the Clos Pegase collection points the answer to wine's preeminent importance.

Watch for these other outstanding features while on tour:

- the winemaker's laboratory, a little masterpiece of practical contemporary architecture and built-in cabinetry bathed in northeastern light
- the three-hundred-year-old oak tree framed by the two axes of the winery
- terra-cotta tiles covering the winery's floor, lending unity with the Greco-Roman building style; there's even a wine gutter cut into the tiles along the tasting room floor
- the tall barrels beyond the tasting room window wall, reproductions of wine-aging vats found in ancient Roman drawings; they were constructed of French oak in the United States
- the massive single column that dominates the entrance to the winery. Is it supportive or purely an artistic statement?

A number of visitors are curious about the winery's name. Why Pegasus as a "mascot?" Shrem's response is that he and his wife wished to reflect the mythological beginning of wine. According to the legends, Pegasus, the winged horse of Greek mythology, gave birth to wine and the arts when his hooves unleashed the sacred Spring of the Muses. The spring waters tapped roots of the vines and thus inspired the artists and poets who drank the fruit of the vine.

"*Clos*," in French, connotes any enclosed space. As a Napa Valley winery, Clos Pegase is not just any enclosed space—it is unique.

CODORNIU NAPA

The sleek, contemporary elements of Codorniu Napa are hidden in the heart of a grassy hill. This, one of Napa Valley's newest wineries, was designed to reproduce the form of a previously existing knoll in the Carneros vineyard region. Besides incurring minimal impact on the countryside, the winery's design harmonizes—in fact meshes—with the surrounding landscape.

The Codorniu family of Barcelona has produced wine since 1551 and was the first family in Spain to create *méthode champenoise* sparkling wine, in 1872. With such an ancient history, some might expect Moorish arches and Old World architecture for this, the first sparkling wine-making venture for Codorniu outside its native country. But, after five years of scouting the grape-growing regions of the world, the decision was to buy land in Carneros and to build a sweepingly modern winery. The enterprise has drawn acclaim since its opening in 1991.

To reach the imposing property, you turn off Old Sonoma Road, very near Domaine Carneros. In fact, one suggestion is to visit both wineries back-to-back so that you can experience the variations in style—architectural as well as enological—between the French and the Spanish companies.

On approaching the site, you may have difficulty identifying the estate until you reach the winery sign at the gates. Then comes the great "Aha!"

Yes, the winery is in view all along, but it blends so well with the surroundings that it appears to be one of many other craggy hills in the area. Due as well to the native California matte fescue grasses planted on the earthen berm covering the facility, the winery hides its face. Once you are on the curving drive to the parking area at the base of the winery, Domingo Triay's minimalist architecture becomes a dominating force, which is sure to hold your attention throughout the stay.

A cascading waterfall cuts the center of the forty-five broad steps you will climb to reach Codorniu's entry. The view seems to offer new and better panoramas at each landing during the ascent, culminating in the breathtaking view on the top of the knoll. There you can see the San Francisco Bay in the distance. Nearer is San Pablo Bay, which hugs the edges of Carneros, bringing with it the famous fog of the region. The same view encompasses Millikin Peak and rolling hills and vineyards, including Codorniu's 110 acres of vines. (In order to produce 10,000 cases annually—with the capacity of 180,000 cases annually—Codorniu winemaker Janet Pagano buys Pinot Noir and Chardonnay grapes from neighboring Carneros growers to enhance the winery's grape tonnage.)

From the fountains playing at the winery's promontory, you will walk into the sophisticated silence of the winery. There, surrounded by elegant wood and metal interiors also designed by Triay, you will be warmly greeted and led on a comprehensive tour. The guide will cover history including ancient barrels and other wine-making artifacts brought from Barcelona, and sparkling wine making, which includes viewing the winery's unique conveyor belt press for grapes. Fine art is mounted in the gallery just off the reflecting pool on the main floor, which has changing shows.

Tours tend to be small in size; between six and ten visitors

stroll with the guide. Even if you have entered via the handi-capped access, expect some stairs on the tour. You will not actually descend four stories into the ground, but from an upper walkway you will see the aging sparkling wine on pallets. (For a complete discussion of the process of making sparkling wine, please see the chapter on Schramsberg Vineyards.)

There is something at this winery for everyone. You can choose to learn about the technical side of the winery or you may sit on the veranda, sip sparkling brut and bask in the view.

The Spanish have a saying for it: *"Que vida tan allegre!"*— what a happy life!

Cuvaison Winery

4550 Silverado Trail
Calistoga, CA 94515
(707) 942-6266;
telefax (707) 942-5732

Winemaker: John Thatcher
Winery owner:
Alexander Schmidheiny

Access

Location: From Highway 29, 6 miles north of St. Helena and 2 miles south of Calistoga, take Dunaweal Lane to the Silverado Trail. Turn right; the winery is 500 yards ahead on the left.

Hours open for visits and tastings: 10 A.M.–5 P.M. daily, except New Year's Day, Easter (half day), Thanksgiving, and Christmas.

Appointment necessary for tour? Yes.

Wheelchairs accommodated? Yes.

Tastings

Charge for tasting with tour? $3, which includes logo glass; not deductible from price of purchased wine.

Charge for tasting without tour? $3, as above.

Typical wines offered: Chardonnay, Cabernet Sauvignon, Merlot, Pinot Noir, Reserve Chardonnay (all offered as available).

Sales of wine-related items? Yes.

Picnics and Programs

Picnic area open to the public? Yes.

Special events or wine-related programs? Yes.

There is an unassuming quality about Cuvaison Winery. It sits hillside on the Silverado Trail in view of Sterling and around the knoll from Clos Pegase. Three dormant volcanos are within sight—Mount St. Helena, Mount George, and the Mayacamas. Oaks and evergreens border the mission-style winery and a stand of picnic tables awaits warm weather use. In winter, a wood-burning stove in the visitors' center offers a toasty welcome.

Since it opened in 1970, the winery has evolved at an even pace. As a result, an occasional visit can give the sense of observing a favorite nephew sprouting from an elfin kindergartener to a complex young man. Compared to a visit at a venerable winery, this is like a work in progress. For instance, the cozy tasting room and hospitality center that welcome you on entrance to the winery property used to house the entire winery facility, in the early seventies. Then, Cuvaison was a new tax write-off for the two engineers who owned it. Another sign of evolution includes activity in the building that houses fermentation tanks—it is now jammed to the walls with equipment, and outside, six-by-six-foot Pinot Noir tanks have sprouted like Topsy on the back driveway, as winemaker John Thatcher increases his interest in Pinot Noir.

The winery is now quite successful, based on years of radical change and strong management. In 1979 a new owner—Alexander Schmidheiny, of Switzerland, whose family owns Swatch watches and Tobler chocolates, among other concerns—brought a renewed sense of dedication to Cuvaison. And Manfred Esser, the company president, has meshed his own love of food with the marketing of wine in novel ways.

Thatcher has replanted hillside vines with Rutherford-area grapes from the Napa Valley floor. The result has been a move from tannic wines best enjoyed in the future to wines drinkable now as well as able to be laid down.

What is most interesting about touring Cuvaison (which translates from French as "the fermenting of juice on the grape skins in order to extract color") is the sense of seeing evolution in action. In 1992, a new vineyard was planted to offer visitors a chance both to observe various trellising techniques for vine maintenance and to pick and taste grapes during harvest.

Most wineries with memorable tours are relatively large, and their tour styles are quite established. Cuvaison is more informal, beginning with its welcoming approach. The background music in the hospitality room is usually light rock or jazz. The tour guides have been affiliated with the winery for years, and they impart information with a relaxed style, on subjects including winery production and how to read the chalk identification notes scratched on French oak barrels.

As an unusual touch, tourists are given a taste of wine right out of a fermentation vat. Other wineries might offer a barrel tasting, but Cuvaison tour guides open the spigot alongside a vertical tank and pour right into the glass.

"Most of our barrels are housed in two other warehouses in St. Helena and Napa," points out tour guide Janet Behr as the tour passes metal gantries (pallets) holding top-grade French oak barrels. Near the barrel storage area the bottling line rattles along, with views onto the valley through the work station windows.

From watching the bottling action—literally within reach on the tour—you'll move to the wine library, a sophisticated corridor of a room with hundreds of Cuvaison bottles resting in diamond-shaped wooden shelving. The lighting is subtle and the room lends itself to final questions related to the tour. The tour's progression from the simple beginnings of the original winery to the modern surroundings of the wine library seems appropriate for this winery, which continues to reach ever-higher goals.

DOMAINE CARNEROS

Domaine Carneros

1240 Duhig Road
Napa, CA 94559
(707) 257-0101;
telefax (707) 257-3020

Winemaker: Eileen Crane
Winery owners: Champagne
Taittinger, Kobrand and other
American partners

Access
Location: On Route 12/121
(Carneros Highway) at Duhig Road,
4 miles southwest of Napa.

Hours open for visits and tastings:
10:30 A.M. to 6 P.M. daily, except
Thanksgiving, Christmas, and
New Year's Day. Tours: Weekdays:
11 A.M., 1 P.M., and 3 P.M.
Weekends: on the hour between
11 A.M.–3 P.M.

Appointment necessary for tour?
No, except for groups of 12 or more.

Wheelchairs accommodated? Yes.

Tastings
Charge for tasting with tour?
$4 Brut Cuvee, $5 Blanc de Blancs,
$6 Famous Gate Pinot Noir
(when available), not deductible
from price of purchased bottle.

Charge for tasting without tour?
As above.

Typical wines offered for tasting:
Brut Cuvee, Blanc de Blancs.
When available: Blanc de Noirs,
Rose, and Famous Gate Pinot Noir

Sales of wine-related items? Yes.

Picnics and Programs
Picnic area open to the public? No

Special events or wine-related
programs? Food and wine pairing
luncheons, receptions, dinners and
vineyard tours by appointment
(extension 122).

The classic elegance of the eighteenth century-style chateau that houses Domaine Carneros' sparkling wine-making facility draws instant attention from travelers in the southwestern tip of the Carneros district of the Napa Valley. Here, in an area frequently blanketed by fog from nearby San Pablo Bay, the modern castle presides on a hill at the vineyard edge. Among American vineyards, it is an international nexus.

Domaine Carneros itself is a partnership of the Taittinger Champagne house of Reims, France, as well as Kobrand Corporation and other partners. The grapes grown immediately to the north, on René di Rosa's property, are used in making Winery Lake and Sterling vintages for Seagram, the Canadian spirits company. Spain holds forth behind the di Rosa property; almost out of view due to its minimalist architecture, Codorniu Napa's profile hints to those who search the hills. Finally, south of Domaine Carneros lie the Swiss vineyards of Cuvaison.

Since the first area infusion of French funds, with the purchase of Domaine Chandon in 1973, the Napa Valley has seen major construction and growth owing to its international support. In most cases, the recently built wineries have demonstrated modern architectural styling. But in the case of Domaine Carneros this is not so.

This winery is patterned after the Taittinger-owned Chateau de la Marquetterie in Champagne. Seventy-two steps, broken by occasional landings, lead to the broad stone terrace and entry of the winery. (There is a clearly-designated secondary entrance for those intimidated by the stairway.) The first impression once inside is of the grandeur of the place: high ceilings, a graceful staircase, and well-appointed furnishings balance with local limestone and French marble floors.

Follow your eyes into the tasting room at the north wing of the "chateau." It is there that you will join a tour group to see the inner workings of the winery, as well as to learn the background on the French link with Domaine Carneros.

"The fireplace mantel is a Louis XVI piece brought from France, as is this painting of Madame de Pompadour, mistress of Louis XV," says the tour guide. The story goes that a fortune-teller alerted Madame de Pompadour's father that his daughter was to be the mistress of the king. As a result, the gentleman trained his daughter for life in court. That meant he made certain she knew how to read and write in order to mesh easily with the literate lords and ladies of Louis XV's inner circle. This painting, which commands the foyer and which formerly hung at the Hotel Crillon in Paris, depicts Madame de Pompadour with books and sheet music.

From that historical discussion, you will move into a video presentation about the vineyard year for Pinot Noir and Chardonnay, the two grapes ideal for sparkling wine. An excellent segment explains the budding process used on the rootstock. At the video's conclusion, the wide screen is raised and behind a large window you will see a "forest" of stainless steel fermentation tanks, a practical extension of the wine-making procedures covered on film.

From there, a short staircase leads down to a viewing platform from which the guide will point out the continuing stages of *méthode champenoise*, the double-fermentation sparkling-wine process that creates effervescence in the wine. This includes riddling, which primarily is done by mechanical

methods despite winemaker Eileen Crane's inclusion of hand-riddling at the winery. You'll also see the disgorging, dosage, corking, cleaning, neck-foiling, labeling, and bottling line, which is extremely modern equipment in comparison with the antique bottlers on display on the platform.

"Remember," laughs the guide, "the lower the alcohol content, the lower the calories—and sparkling wine has a total of only 12 percent alcohol. I call it a sumptuous diet drink!"

As the group follows along, they learn that ultraviolet light prematurely ages sparkling wine, which is why the aging area—where the wine is aged twenty months—is rather dimly lit. Because the winery was built on top of a knoll, the temperature in the underground aging area simulates cave temperature. This architectural technique frequently is employed to reduce air-conditioning costs as much as to effect cavelike conditions.

In the design of this opulent setting, even the restrooms received detailed attention. These are the best-appointed restrooms in the valley.

Back upstairs, Domaine Carneros wine is sold by the glass or by the bottle, accompanied by tasty appetizers. Despite formal surroundings, the tasting-room staff is warm and genial.

There is a sense of the civilized life that arises from sitting on French-style chairs, listening to classical music, and sipping Napa Valley sparkling wine, overlooking the hills of Carneros. Whether you visit wearing jeans or summer finery, be prepared to feel like royalty.

DOMAINE CHANDON

Domaine Chandon

1 California Drive
Yountville, CA 94599
(707) 944-2280;
telefax (707) 944-1123
Restaurant: 800-736-2892

Winemaker: Dawnine Dyer
Winery owner:
Moët-Hennessey–Louis Vuitton

Access

Location: Off Highway 29 at
Yountville. From the Veterans Home
exit, southwest on California Drive;
turn right.

Hours open for visits and tastings:
11 A.M.–5 P.M. May through
October, open daily; November
through April, closed Mondays and
Tuesdays. Call for restaurant hours.
Tours given on the hour between
11 A.M. and 5 P.M. No charge
for tours.

Appointment necessary for tour?
No, except for groups of 16 or more.

Wheelchairs accommodated? Yes.

Tastings

Charge for tasting with tour? Yes.

Charge for tasting without tour? Yes.

Sparkling wines may be purchased
by the glass or by the bottle in the
tasting salon.

Typical wines offered: Brut,
Blanc de Noir, Reserve.

Sales of wine-related items? Yes.

Picnics and Programs

Picnic area open to the public?
No (restaurant on property).

Special events or wine-related
programs? Quarterly newsletter;
also the Chandon Club, offering
special events and other benefits.

The marriage of past and present in a Napa Valley winery is best demonstrated at Domaine Chandon, on the western side of Yountville, with its sparkling-wine facility and restaurant. It seems appropriate that this town, named for George C. Yount, who planted the first Napa Valley grape rootstock in 1838, would be home to another innovation—the first French-owned California winery.

Moët-Hennessey-Louis Vuitton is today's name for the massive French holding company that took a chance in 1973 and purchased vineyard land in three Napa Valley areas—Yountville, the Mount Veeder hills, and Carneros. The goal of the company and master winemaker Edmund Maudière was to grow Chardonnay, Pinot Noir, and Pinot Blanc grapes for sparkling-wine production. Simultaneously, the company decided to open a restaurant of high caliber where the sparkling wines, as well as other Napa Valley still wines, would be presented in an ideal setting for food and wine.

None of the dedication to excellence has decreased since the 1977 opening. Over time, numerous ancient French Champagne-making implements have been installed along the broad walkways leading from the stone-and-cement contemporary-style hospitality center to the modern wine-making complex, linking the French roots even more visibly.

Near the landscaped entry road an abstract fountain plays in one of the man-made ponds. Across the wooden footbridge is an underground hub of tourist activity. There you will find a well-designed display on cooperage (barrel making) and one on glass bottle making that includes an excellent visual on the various sizes of Champagne bottles from the 187-milliliter smallest to the fifteen-liter Nebuchadnezzar. Some visitors walk up the interior cement steps and head for the restaurant; others choose to go directly to the salon at the head of the stairs where they can sit at tables and purchase sparkling wine or Panache, the winery's aperitif wine. Appetizers are served as well.

The majority of tourists congregate downstairs for the half-hour walking tour of the winery. Although the Grand Central Station noise level tends to mask the tour guide's opening remarks, the basic elements of the tour are friendly, educational, and performed with style. Tour groups are large here—thirty to forty visitors—but the guides have an unin-timidating manner that invites questions from novices and experts. Photography is encouraged. Expect a good number of steps on this tour, as the facilities are built on different levels.

There is a thrill similar to discovering a secret in walking the area lined with rows of fourteen-thousand-gallon stainless steel fermentation tanks. Eloquent guides such as Maria Monti describe the *méthode champenoise* procedure of in-bottle fermentation, assisted by clear graphics, which demonstrate the movement of the "yeast smear" sediment of dead yeast. This yeast collects in the bottle and then is manipulated by riddling down into the bottle's neck for easy removal. In the riddling area, to which you descend, two hundred thousand bottles of wine rest their necks in wooden riddling racks, waiting silently for daily quarter-turns.

Within the Napa Valley, there is some confusion concerning the naming of sparkling wines. Some wineries call it Champagne; others dub it Napa Valley Champagne; and

"sparkling wine" is used by many. Actually, all forms of nomenclature are legally correct. The Treaty of Madrid stated that only sparkling wine from the Champagne region of France could hold that name. European countries signed the agreement in 1890, and as a result, Spain calls its sparkling wine *cava*, Italy calls it *spumanti*, and Germany names it *sekt*. However, the United States never signed, on the principle that our "don't tread on me" attitude should not yield to such a dictate from Europe. Also, the later experience of Prohibition made the concept of sparkling wine produced in this country unthinkable. In any case, Domaine Chandon defers to the treaty's ruling because of the company's French parentage. Ergo, this sparkling wine is called just that.

To keep up with the high volume production of Domaine Chandon's Brut, Blanc de Noirs, Reserve, Première, Etoile, and Club Cuvée sparkling styles, very large machines (amusingly called VLMs) riddle hundreds of bottles simultaneously, creating the same small beads (bubbles) as the hand-riddled wine.

"Is it true," asks a tourist, "that the larger the bubbles the larger the headache?" The guide responds that large beads are called toad's eyes and that she believes there is some truth to the tale, although it has not been proven. She is quick to point out that the froth of bubbles atop a freshly poured glass of sparkling wine is called a mousse and not a head. "That's another beverage," she states with a smile.

Back upstairs you'll view the entire final wine processing system from an upper platform. The stages of activity are well marked, so that the process is clear, even at the noisy peak of disgorging, corking, and bottle-tumbling to final foiling, labeling, and boxing of the bottles.

Given a dormant bottling line, the tour guide will use the quiet platform area to demonstrate how to properly open a bottle of sparkling wine. Basic information is given, such as, "Chill it three hours in the refrigerator or at least forty minutes in an ice bucket," as well as sparkling-wine trivia; the speed at which a cork exits the bottle (sixty-two miles per hour) and how many counterclockwise turns will release the wire cage on any sparkling-wine bottle in the world (six and one-half).

Good-byes are said alongside the Beaujolais horizontal-style press, which was used from 1600 through the late 1800s. Appropriately, the press is mounted near an imposing modern stone arch.

Without question, this winery blends the old and the new with strong touches of education and hospitality.

FLORA SPRINGS WINERY

Flora Springs Winery
1978 West Zinfandel Lane
St. Helena, CA 94574
(707) 963-5711;
telefax (707) 963-7518

Winemaker: Kenneth Deis

Winery owners:
The Komes and Garvey Families

Access
Location: At the south end of
St. Helena, off Highway 29. Turn
west on Zinfandel Lane; proceed
to the end of Zinfandel, and turn
right where the road forks.

Hours open for visits and tastings:
10 A.M.–4 P.M. Monday through
Thursday; 10 A.M.–3 P.M. Friday
and Saturday, except Easter,
Memorial Day, Fourth of July,
Thanksgiving, Christmas, and
New Year's Day.

Appointment necessary for tour? Yes.

Wheelchairs accommodated?
Yes, in tasting room; not on tour.

Tastings
Charge for tasting with tour?
No, except that bus tours of large
groups are $5 per person.

Charge for tasting without tour? No.

Typical wines offered: Barrel
Fermented Chardonnay, Merlot,
Cabernet Sauvignon, Trilogy,
Soliloquy, San Giovese.

Sales of wine-related items?
Yes, including logo glasses ($3).

Picnics and Programs
Picnic area open to the public? No.

Special events or wine-related
programs? Kitchen and dining room
available for catered meals.
Minimum 25 guests, maximum 45.

Ancient oak, pine, and olive trees edge the property of Flora Springs Winery, which hugs the western hillsides along the south end of St. Helena and then spreads across the valley floor. Many of those very trees shaded the periphery of this 250-acre property in the 1880s when Scotsmen William and James Rennie built the winery that is still in use today, with another family at its hub.

The majority of the Zinfandel Lane property stretches north and east, yielding a magnificent valley view. This was the same view Louis M. Martini chose as his personal panorama when he bought the land in 1930 to create his private estate, where he lived until his death in 1974.

The winery remained dormant three years until Jerry and Flora Komes purchased the property in 1977 as a "retirement getaway," using the Swiss chalet-style home Martini had built in 1956 as the family headquarters. In brief time, many of the Komes' adult children joined their parents in realizing the wine-making potential, moving to the Napa Valley to bring reality to their dreams. In 1979, Chardonnay was the first wine aged and bottled by Flora Springs. As a result of the team effort in creating the wine, this is one of the most active family-owned wineries in the valley.

Some details at the winery seem dichotomous: two gas pumps face the ivy-covered building, adding a down-home touch to the nearby terra-cotta-colored arches neatly framing terraces of brilliantly hued flowers. And a graceful old oak tree surrounded by generous wooden benches faces a tiled plaza—without a seat in sight—outside the tasting room. Within the cool, newly furbished tasting room, there are plenty of tables and chairs.

While visiting the winery, you are guided on an excellent vineyard visit. At the opening of the tour, you walk on gravel the size of large peas from the huge oak to the vineyard. There, some explanation is given on canopy management, which relates to the various trellis systems used on the property. At this location and throughout the Napa Valley, leafy vines are propped on metal supports or strung on wires in

the shape of a T or a Y or a U. Vinyardists choose to so arrange vines in order to control sunlight, any mildew on the plants, and the development of the fruit. On the other hand, many vines grow in the old-fashioned, non-trellised method, with their branches billowing to the earth.

There is an area visited at the commencement of the tour that offers a lesson in viticultural management. The lesson is best understood midsummer, when leaves and young berries (grapes) crowd the vines. What you will see is about ten rows of Merlot vines on vertical trellises where sun is relatively filtered over hills and through branches of the hillside trees. Those westernmost vines clearly produce fewer leaves and grapes, due measurably to the diminished amount of sunlight. No wonder most vineyards are maintained in the full sun of the valley floor.

Watch for "Organic Farming Trials" signs as you cross the entry road over to the Cabernet Sauvignon vineyards. There is a small, growing contingent of winemakers experimenting with organic plantings by eliminating pesticides; Flora Springs is one of that group.

Questions on organic gardening methods can lead to other queries. With 90 percent of Napa Valley vines due to be affected by the phylloxera strain of root louse, many visitors' questions lean toward the result of such infestation and how it is being treated. The winery guides here answer all questions knowledgeably: "What does it cost to treat and replant an acre of vineyard when it is hit by phylloxera?"—"Twenty-five to thirty thousand dollars."

"How many years has phylloxera been in the Napa Valley?"—"It was here in the 1880s, then that strain was eradicated. This mutant strain survives on AXR1, a rootstock that was believed to be impermeable to root louse until now."

And a simple question, related to a commonly sighted item: "Why all the milk cartons at the bases of the young vines?"—"Rabbits love tender vine shoots and they are repelled by the waxy boxes."

Flora Springs grapes are hand-harvested from a total of 450 acres. (There are four other vineyard locations separate from this Zinfandel Lane property.) The fruit is crushed in the bladder presses arranged in front of fifteen gleaming stainless steel tanks outside the old winery. While you stand outside near the crush pad, the wine-making process is clearly explained, from grape picking to barrel aging to bottling. Then a walk up a circular staircase leads to a view of the wine aging barrels and a walk through the old winery's interior.

Merlot, the winery cat, may pad by. The guide points out some necessities of life in the country: "The cat keeps down the mice, and bats keep down the bugs." Four hundred and fifty French oak barrels with "medium toast" rest on site, with 50 percent of the barrels new at any time. Watch for a few French upright barrels (1200-gallon capacity) and German uprights (1600 gallons).

Although the winery is not built in a cave, the temperature remains cool, due to the thick stone walls and the natural air conditioning caused by ivy growing along the walls of the building. As the ivy transpires it gives its moisture to the building, even on the hottest of days.

Once the tour wends its way to the tasting room, the guide will demonstrate the preferred parts of a wine glass to hold when drinking wine (the base or the stem), as well as how to check for wine clarity, methods for swirling wine in the glass (volatizing the esters), and how to taste wine to best advantage. The emphasis is on enjoying wine with food— such vintages as Flora Springs' Trilogy, an example of the new "Meritage" wines, that is a blend of Cabernet Sauvignon, Cabernet Franc, and Merlot juices.

Due to the friendliness of the tour guides, there is usually a sense of openness and well being among the winery visitors by the end of the hour-long tour and tasting, and even talk among some about return visits in following years.

Freemark Abbey Winery

3022 St. Helena Highway
St. Helena, CA 94574
(707) 963-9694;
telefax (707) 963-0554

Winemaker: Ted Edwards
Winery owner: Partnership:
Charles Carpy, Managing Partner

Access

Location: Approximately 2 miles
north of St. Helena at Highway 29
and Lodi Lane.

Hours open for visits and tastings:
May–October, 10 A.M.–4:30 P.M.
daily, Tour 2 P.M. November–April,
10 A.M.–4:30 P.M. daily,
Tour 2 P.M., no tours or tastings
on Monday.

Appointment necessary for tour?
Yes, for other than 2 P.M. tour.

Wheelchairs accommodated? Yes.

Tastings

Charge for tasting with tour? $3.

Charge for tasting without tour? $3.

Typical wines offered: Four to five
wines; typically one white and three
reds, including a reserve or library
Cabernet Sauvignon.

Sales of wine-related items? Yes.
Tasting fee includes logo glass.

Picnics and Programs

Picnic area open to the public?
No, private functions only.

Special events or wine-related
programs? Not regularly scheduled,
but winery does host private wine
dinners.

Just north of St. Helena, Freemark Abbey offers tourists the quiet blend of a century-old stone winery and a modern wine tasting room. Winter is my favorite season to visit this winery, due to the warm homecoming feeling evoked by the roaring fire in the stone fireplace and the living room quality of the tasting room. There's a baby grand piano in a corner of the room, just beyond the fringes of an oriental carpet, and comfortable armchairs and sofas beckon to the traveler.

Freemark Abbey traces its origins to 1886 and to the first woman to build and operate a California winery. Josephine Tychson's home still exists as a private residence just across Highway 29 on Tychson Road. During the tour you'll hear about her struggles as a young widow managing the vineyards and overseeing the building of the native quarry stone winery. At that time, much of the labor was done by Chinese workers who lived in Calistoga—their pickax marks are still visible inside the winery.

A side note: If the Victorian era history of the area fascinates you, don't miss the Sharpsteen Museum on Washington Street in Calistoga. There you'll see dioramas and exact representations of the town as it was when well-to-do San Franciscans traveled by ferry to Vallejo and then by train to Calistoga, where they bathed in the famous restorative mineral waters of the region. The museum includes photos of the "China camp" where laborers lived in community.

In 1905, Anton Forni, the mayor of St. Helena, bought Freemark Abbey. Later he sold it to Albert Ahern. Despite the seeming monastic style of its title, the winery's name actually derives from Ahern's nickname, Abbey, and from the names of two friends, Freeman and Mark.

Today, the guided winery tour winds through the French doors of the tasting room onto a terrace with a view of the gardens and lawn fronting the original winery. As you walk along the vineyards and then down a gentle slope to view the crush pad area, the guide will explain that in 1966 Chuck Carpy, a grape grower and native St. Helenan, partnered with renowned vineyard manager Laurie Wood and five other men who were active in the community. That group worked to renovate Freemark Abbey, which had been relatively dormant for years. "The first thing we had to do was completely renovate the lower cellars," recalls Carpy. "There were dirt floors, some dirt walls, and the cooperage was shot. Most of the old casks were pre-Prohibition." A year later they brought in their first vintage, and they have retained their partnership ever since.

Be sure to wear sweaters in the cellars—the two-foot-thick walls keep the temperature at fifty-five degrees, plus or minus one or two degrees, ideal for storing wine. While in the cellar you'll learn how to decipher the winemaker's cryptic notes on the sixty-gallon Nevers barrels. You'll also probably meet the cellarmaster, Ignacio Delgadillo, unless the harvest, which yields around 36,000 cases of wine, is at its peak.

There is a candle shop and a couple of restaurants at the winery entrance, which can make this a full afternoon stop.

Grgich Hills Cellars

1829 St. Helena Highway
Rutherford, CA 94573
(707) 963-2784;
telefax (707) 963-8725

Winemaker: Miljenko "Mike" Grgich
Winery owners:
Miljenko Grgich and Austin Hills

Access

Location: On Highway 29, ½ mile
north of Rutherford, on the west
side of the highway.

Hours open for visits and tastings:
9:30 A.M.–4:30 P.M. daily, except
Easter, Good Friday (half day),
Thanksgiving, Christmas, and
New Year's Day.

Appointment necessary for tour?
Yes; check winery for times of the
two tours a day.

Wheelchairs accommodated?
Yes, except in restrooms.

Tastings

Charge for tasting with tour?
On weekends and holidays only,
$2 for each glass; not deductible
from price of purchased wine.

Charge for tasting without tour?
As above.

Typical wines offered: Chardonnay,
Fumé Blanc, Zinfandel, Cabernet
Sauvignon, and Late Harvest
Johannisberg Riesling.

Sales of wine-related items? Yes.

Picnics and Programs

Picnic area open to the public? No.

Special events or wine-related
programs? The Pre-Release Club,
which entitles members to early
notification of new wines and also
an annual festival. Discounts on
wines through the club.

At a time when U.S. wine marketing is based generally on wine with food, Miljenko "Mike" Grgich is a man whose winery is doing something specific about it.

The tour at Grgich Hills Cellars may involve a discussion of the link between wine making and food preparation, with specific examples to show the similarities. Take chicken stock. At home, you can make a delicious stock by combining essential base ingredients—at least chicken, onion, carrots, celery, and salt—in a pot with water, bringing it to a boil and then letting the rich flavors steep into the liquid during a slow simmer. You skim fats and residues that float to the surface or, for further refining, you can stir foamy egg whites into the broth as a "food magnet" to attract and hold tiny food particles. A fine sieve can then remove those impurities.

While standing in the award-bedecked tasting room, the knowledgeable Grgich guide explains how wine making is a similar series of activities. By combining flavor bases—grapes from various vineyards picked at different times and temperatures—and allowing the grapes to sit together, you induce fermentation and a cap of residue forms. The cap is then strained off and the fermented grape juice is refined, often with the help of egg whites, and bottled as wine, one of the few living, breathing, fermenting beverages.

"Wine is a living thing," the knowledgeable tour guide explains; "It will change over time because it is alive. Not so for spirits, which will never change."

The tour moves from the overly dark tasting room where it begins into the day's brilliance back at the winery's entry, and on to the edge of one of the early Grgich Hills vineyards paralleling Highway 29. There you'll learn that all the grapes are picked by hand, a dictate from the two men who own the winery. Mike Grgich is also the winemaker, having immigrated from Croatia with a strong desire to make wine; Austin Hills, the winery's co-owner, is an heir to the Hills Brothers coffee fortune. Hills jumped at the chance of partnership with Grgich immediately after the 1976 Paris "crowning" of the '73 Chateau Montelena Chardonnay, when he was winemaker there. Grgich had taken enology studies at the University of Zagreb and still wears a student beret.

As a winery to visit, Grgich Hills is ideal for connoisseurs and for those who wish to learn about wine making. You'll learn such tips as how to differentiate American oak barrels from French ones (American barrels have a narrow belly compared to the French, which can hold as much as 3.3 gallons more wine).

Why use oak barrels? The guide will explain that there's a

biochemical interchange of phenol from the oak into the aging wine, which adds more flavor to the final product.

During a walk through the wine-making facility, you will see a number of cold stabilization tanks jacketed in ice. Mike Grgich filters 70 percent of his wines using this increasingly popular method of refining the fermented juice. A difference in his use of the method is that no further filters or diatomaceous earth are used. The concept is that other filters can add their own problems to already refined wine.

The wine tasting conducted for the tour takes place separated from the interior tasting room. On a sunny day, you may sit outside in leafy shade under the trees or the redwood trellis. Only the hum of traffic on Highway 29 will distract as you and the other guests in your group sip Napa Valley Chardonnay, and other varietals while learning how to taste wine and how to compare vintages.

Each time I have toured Grgich, the guide has mentioned that the winery philosophy is moving away from corks as a method of bottle closure, considering plastic caps and metal screwcaps. Although this may seem odd here in the realm of corkscrews (and the winery hasn't made a switch yet), Mike Grgich is known as a futurist within the industry.

Chances are you'll see Mike Grgich as you travel around the winery—watch for the man in a beret. If he is able to put his projects on hold, he'll happily answer your wine-making questions, adding to the wealth of understanding you will have gained from the tour.

The Hess Collection Winery

4411 Redwood Road
Napa, CA 94558
(707) 255-1144;
telefax (707) 253-1682

Winemaker: Randle Johnson
Winery owner: Donald Hess

Access

Location: Heading north on Highway 29 to the town of Napa, make a left on Redwood Road at its intersection with Trancas. Continue west about 6 miles to the winery.

Hours open for visits and tastings: 10 A.M.–4 P.M. daily, except Easter, Fourth of July, Thanksgiving, Christmas, and New Year's Day.

Appointment necessary for tour? No. Self-guided tours only for groups of up to 12 people.

Wheelchairs accommodated? Yes.

Tastings

Charge for tasting with tour? $2.50; not deductible from price of purchased wine.

Charge for tasting without tour? As above.

Typical wines offered: Current releases of Chardonnay and Cabernet Sauvignon.

Sales of wine-related items? Yes, including museum catalog.

Picnics and Programs

Picnic area open to the public? No.

Special events or wine-related programs? Private dinners for up to 100 people.

Redwood Road winds along the southwestern hills of Napa, leading you through shaded forests of sequoias and fields of mountain wildflowers. Solitary hawks glide effortlessly, dotting clear blue skies with their graceful form. There is a subtle similarity here to driving circuitous routes in the Sierra foothills. Without question, this road is Northern California at its best.

With such a dramatic approach as Redwood Road leading to the Hess Collection Winery and museum, you might predict a lesser experience at road's end. But the truth is that the adventure only advances.

Walking from the parking area to the winery, you'll pass a sculpture garden and then face two splendid stone structures, merged with an internal spine of clean, contemporary architecture. The main building was constructed around 1903 as Mount La Salle, home for Northern California Christian Brothers. Once inside, you'll experience airy spaciousness. There is a mix of turn-of-the-century stonework and quiet modern lines that acts as a background for art and a stage for winery procedures.

The gratis tour here is self-guided and incorporates elements of the art of wine making with a museum of contemporary paintings and sculptures that are mounted in a thirteen-thousand-square-foot gallery. Visitors have the opportunity to view works by Frank Stella, Robert Motherwell, Magdalena Abakanowicz, Francis Bacon, and other world-renowned artists. This museum is winery owner Donald Hess's "gift to the public." Hess is a Swiss-American ninth-generation brewmaster based in Bern. There he headquarters a variety of companies including Valser St. Petersquelle, the second-largest brand of mineral water in Switzerland; an alpine trout hatchery; and eighteen restaurants.

Hess believed that with his vineyards as well as his Hess Collection Winery and museum on Mount Veeder, an extinct volcano in the Mayacamas Range, his grapes would fare well—due to the stress of surviving in the rocky soil of the Mount Veeder appellation. He had good reason. Although a visit to the hilly vineyards is not possible, they can be viewed in two ways: stop at one of the gallery's dormer windows and glance at the promontory across the way. You may see workers pruning the vines. Or take a few minutes to view the nine-projector slide show in the small theater on the winery's second floor. The seats are as comfortable as the plushest lodge accommodation, and the room is a cool respite on a scorching day.

The slide presentation is the finest of any I have seen in the industry. The images take you through the 130-day push in the grape growing cycle. Pictures and music highlight seasonal changes while they introduce the people, techniques, and equipment necessary to make fine wine.

On exiting the theater, you can't miss Leopold Malers's *Hommage 1974*, a flaming typewriter with a powerful image.

After the self-guided tour (with easy access by stairway or elevator), pass the massive floral arrangement on the first floor and proceed to the tasting room and its adjacent retail room. There you'll find a huge wooden bar in a room surrounded by stone walls and aging barrels. The room's warm tones contrast with the gallery's brightness. The hosts and hostesses can answer any wine-making or tasting questions about the winery's Cabernet Sauvignons and Chardonnays.

My guess is that this winery visit will be one of the most memorable of your Napa Valley tour.

Charles Krug Winery

2800 Main Street
St. Helena, CA 94574
(707) 967-2201;
telefax (707) 967-2293

Winemaker: John Moynier
Winery owner: Peter Mondavi & Sons

Access

Location: North of St. Helena on Highway 29's northeast side between the "tunnel of trees" and Deer Park Road.

Hours open for visits and tastings: 10:30 A.M.–5:30 P.M. daily. Closed Easter, Thanksgiving, Christmas Eve, Christmas, and New Year's Day. Tours given daily except Wednesdays.

Appointment necessary for tour? No.

Wheelchairs accommodated? Yes.

Tastings

Charge for tasting with tour? $1; in exchange, each tourist receives one Krug Buck to be used toward purchase.

Charge for tasting without tour? $3 for five wines, which includes a logo glass, $3 fee waived on Wednesdays; or $6 for five vertical vintage selection Cabernets, which also includes a logo glass.

Typical wines offered: Cabernet Sauvignon, Chardonnay, and at least two other varietals.

Sales of wine-related items? Yes, a wide variety.

Picnics and Programs

Picnic area open to the public? Yes.

Special events or wine-related programs? A series of invitational "Tastings on the Lawn" is offered as an annual event. New releases are offered along with cheese and music. August Moon concerts are held annually. For information about special events, call 707-967-2245.

One of the best vineyard tours in the Napa Valley is offered at the Charles Krug Winery. Actually, this should be the case, considering the fact that Krug, founded in 1861, is the oldest winery in the valley. Numerous excellent winemakers have apprenticed and worked in the twelve-hundred-acre vineyard, and the tradition of reverence for the land is apparent during the tour.

On a midweek afternoon, you can expect to share the vineyard and production facility tour with people from all over the world, as the wine has international recognition.

A favorite time of year to visit the winery is late spring, when mustard flowers make the approach to the winery a sea of yellow blossoms and dogwoods add pink and white touches along distant hills, with Mount St. Helena, a formerly active volcano to the north, rising 4300 feet above the pastel valley floor. From the parking area looking west, there is also an outstanding view of Greystone Cellars, the imposing stone building that earlier housed The Christian Brothers wine cellars. Now that structure is the new home of the Culinary Institute of America Center for Advanced Studies.

Considering the history and glamor of Charles Krug Winery's past, the welcoming area is friendly in an under-stated way. But the true reason to tour this winery is to learn the stages of the life of wine grapes from the vineyard point of view. Knowledgeable tour guides use down-to-earth language in describing such stages as "bud break" (the first sign of buds in spring), "veraison" (grape skin coloration), and "Brix" (related to the sugar level of grapes).

"Bud break," explained one Charles Krug guide, "happens when the soil temperature is between fifty and fifty-five degrees. Then leaves and flower buds are growing about one inch a week—like a kid with a haircut."

The relatively small number of tourists on the guided walk is a boon when you're walking right into the vineyards. The tour guide is easily heard as he discusses trellising systems for grape vines. During the outdoor visit, the guide will point out that "cordons" are two canes or "arms" that are left to trail from the main trunk of the vine, as opposed to the "kicker cane," which is one cane left from the past year's growth.

Questions are encouraged, no matter how basic. Want to see smudge pots (portable agricultural gas heaters)? No problem—the group moves over to view them, at the request. You'll walk through the production area as well, viewing fermentation tanks and barrels. Since the winery makes fourteen varietals, ranging from White Zinfandel to vintage-

selection Cabernet Sauvignon, some activity is bound to be taking place, no matter what season of the year.

The winery has a rich history, which is discussed at the long wooden tasting bar while at least three wines are offered. It was Charles Krug who founded the winery and was a moving force in the infant Napa Valley wine industry, encouraging some of his assistant winemakers, such as Jacob Beringer, to move out on their own to strengthen the business. Krug was the first in the valley to use a wine press, rather than the foot-stomping method employed until then.

When Krug died, in 1902, a friend held the winery in receivership until Cesare Mondavi brought the winery back to life in 1943. It was from this winery that Robert Mondavi moved to found his own company. And the Charles Krug Winery is still owned and operated by Cesare's son Peter Mondavi and by his sons, Marc and Peter, Jr.

Although the old family home is not open to the public, Krug's hospitality is offered throughout the year during the Harvest Festival and a variety of music performances.

Louis M. Martini Winery

254 South St. Helena Highway
St. Helena, CA 94574
(707) 963-2736;
telefax (707) 963-8750

Winemaker: Michael Martini
Winery owner: The Martini family

Access
Location: South of the St. Helena city limits on the northeast side of Highway 29.

Hours open for visits and tastings: 10 A.M.–4:30 P.M. daily, except Easter, Thanksgiving, Christmas Eve, Christmas, and New Year's Day. Tours given continuously.

Appointment necessary for tour? No.

Wheelchairs accommodated? Yes.

Tastings
Charge for tasting with tour? No.

Charge for tasting without tour? No, except that five reserve wines may be tasted for $5 (includes logo glass); not deductible from price of purchased wine.

Typical wines offered: Varies each month; usually six each day, featuring a Cabernet and a Chardonnay.

Sales of wine-related items? Yes.

Picnics and Programs
Picnic area open to the public? Yes.

Special events or wine-related programs? Yes.

Of all the wineries chosen for this collection, the Louis M. Martini Winery in St. Helena may be the least imposing in appearance. Yet considering the family tradition and the longtime dedication by three generations of Martini winemakers, this establishment is well worth a visit.

The emphasis in the hospitality room is on two walls: one wall is hung with historical and agricultural photos; the facing wall houses a long wooden wine bar. Wine production is the family story, and the tastings here are extensive. Six wines are offered as a daily complimentary tasting, including older, twelve- to eighteen-year-old wines. For a minimal fee you can also taste the winery's reserve wines.

Few wineries in the valley have inventory enough to be able to share such a varied selection of older Zinfandels, Cabernet Sauvignons, and Pinot Noirs. But Martini can: the company was founded in 1922 by Louis M. Martini in Kingsburg, in the San Joaquin Valley. It has consistently held back wine to share with visitors.

The earliest production by Louis M. Martini, during Prohibition, was a grape concentrate for home wine making named "Forbidden Fruit." Now, with production of 240,000 cases and storage capacity of 2.1 million gallons, the wine library here is extremely comprehensive.

There is an open friendliness in the ambiance at Martini. Tourists are encouraged to bring a picnic lunch to enjoy with wine under the sycamore trees in the quiet of the back garden. Tables and benches are available all day in this hideaway garden, one of the Napa Valley secrets.

The winery tour gives a complete overview of the winemaking process, including a close-up of the crush during harvest. Since the family of Martini winemakers has a tradition of innovation, you will view a number of unusual machines that were derived or purchased to enhance the vintners' process over the years. I have heard tour guides say, "We call that the espresso machine," when pointing to a large stainless steel and iron centrifuging machine sporting wheels, spouts, and bulges.

The innovations from the Martinis actually have been considerable. Louis M. Martini was the first winemaker to purchase substantial acreage in the Carneros region for wine grape cultivation. The family also has developed vineyards in Sonoma Valley such as the renowned Monte Rosso Vineyard and other vineyards in the Chiles and Pope valleys in Napa County. Other innovations include Louis's improvements in grape varieties, changes that aided the industry considerably. He also pioneered mechanical harvesting in California, a method now used in about 65 percent of the vineyards.

There are beautiful old wooden doors to watch for as the guide covers the property from the visitors' center to the solera Sherry aging facility and back. Note the pyramid barrel stacks in the aging rooms. There is usually at least one in the tour group who recalls the huge redwood tanks that until recently nearly filled one massive room. When Louis M.'s grandson Michael accepted the responsibility of wine making from his father Louis P. Martini, he decided to increase the use of sixty-gallon French oak barrels in order to age his wines. Then it was good-bye to the huge tanks of old.

Once back in the tasting room, you might notice the wooden structures around the skylights. They have a strong resemblance to the bases of wine presses; it's so typical of the Martini family to bring the direction right back to wine making!

Robert Mondavi Winery

7801 St. Helena Highway
Oakville, CA 94562
(800) MONDAVI or (707) 226-1395;
telefax (707) 963-1007

Winemaker: Tim Mondavi
Winery owner:
The Robert Mondavi family

Access

Location: On Highway 29, ⅛ mile
north of Oakville.

Hours open for visits and tastings:
9 A.M.–5:30 P.M. May–October;
9:30 A.M.–4:30 P.M. November–
April except Thanksgiving,
Christmas, and New Year's Day.

Appointment necessary for tour?
Yes, suggested; preferably in
advance, but sometimes available
the same day.

Wheelchairs accommodated? Yes.

Tastings

Charge for tasting with tour? No.

Charge for tasting without tour? Yes,
per glass; prices vary.

Typical wines offered: Current
vintages of Chardonnay, Cabernet
Sauvignon, Fumé Blanc, Muscato
d'Oro, Pinot Noir. In the reserve
tasting area, as featured by the taste.

Sales of wine-related items? Yes,
including logo glasses ($3.95 for
4 ½ oz. and $6.95 for 11 ½ oz.).

Picnics and Programs

Picnic area open to the public? No.

Special events or wine-related
programs? The Robert Mondavi
Summer Jazz Festival, The Great
Chefs Program (a series of two-to-
three-day guest chef cooking classes
and meals taught/cooked by noted
chefs and other culinary stars; open
to the public), Wine of the Month
discount program, and the Human
Race, a vineyard run.

The entrance to the Robert Mondavi Winery in Oakville is a generous one, much like the spirit of its founder, who has tirelessly led the California wine industry since he founded his family company in 1966. Broad steps lead past a sleek granite bear sculpted by Beniamino Bufano, and as you approach the terrace the massive mission-style arch frames a splendid vista of the western vineyards and hills.

To many who make the pilgrimage to the valley, the Robert Mondavi Winery is mecca, and their hopes of learning about wine are answered here at the winery known, above all others in the Napa Valley, for its excellent tours.

"Let me say that there are as many different wines as there are types of bread or fish in the sea," notes tour guide Kurt Cobbett as he leads a group of twenty-five guests from the visitors' center into the vineyard facing the parking lot. With that opener, Kurt sets the two themes that are clearly elemental to the Robert Mondavi family philosophy: education leads to knowledge and enjoyment, and wine is a natural accompaniment to food.

If you tour during the late summer and at harvest time you'll be encouraged to sample some of the Sauvignon Blanc grapes from the front vineyard, where some discussion on the history of wine will take place. For instance, wine has its roots in the Middle East, where wine vessels dating to 7000 B.C. have been discovered.

It's no wonder why grapes thrive in the dry, desertlike climate of the Napa Valley, where rainfall is typically absent from April through November.

Moving from the vineyard to the crush pad, guests learn that the stemmer-crusher, which looks like a giant cheese grater, is used to separate grapes from their stems before crushing them. Seemingly small details are added during the discussion, such as the tip that Pinot Noir stems are allowed to remain with the grape, whereas Cabernet Sauvignon stems are removed. If you took notes during a Robert Mondavi tour, you could almost go home and make your own vintage; there are no secrets here.

Once inside the fermentation area, which is filled with rows of huge steel tanks, the comparison of wine making and

cooking utensils becomes quite close. "Now, fermentation is nothing more than little cells eating grape juice," explains the guide. "You've got to realize that these steel tanks are like pots and pans in your kitchen. They need to be airtight because air can spoil food or wine; they are easily cleaned, and they should be able to take refrigeration."

"How can a red grape give white wine?" asks one tourist. I've heard Kurt, as well as other Robert Mondavi tour guides, answer by referring to a different fruit: "Think of an apple. It has red skin, white fruit, and clear juice, just like a grape. If we want white wine, we squeeze the juice and remove the skins.

"If we want to make red wine, we would leave the skins in with the juice for a certain amount of time and then press the mixture and strain off the skins."

Due to the simplified explanations of the ancient art of wine making you can finally understand the basic process and see other heads nodding as you walk to the barrel aging area. The tour guide continues to demystify wine making while reviewing serious numbers, such as the fact that the winery holds 45,000 small French oak barrels. Since each sixty-gallon barrel costs $600, barrels come second only to farming costs in winery expenses.

One of the tour's most pleasant walks follows the visit to the technical wine-making wing of the operation. Tourists stroll around the renowned To-Kalon vineyard bordered by rosebushes. The manicured lawn stretches toward the entry; this lawn is the scene of summer evening jazz concerts during which the winery has presented such greats as Ella Fitzgerald and Ray Charles, while visitors picnic on the green. Following the terra-cotta tiles along the lawn's curve, you'll pass the Vineyard Room off the hospitality wing. There the Mondavi family, under the guidance of Margrit Biever (Robert Mondavi's wife), hosts art shows, concerts, and literary presentations in conjunction with its mission to link wine appreciation with recognition of all the arts.

Your group will conclude its tour with an extensive tasting, which once again promotes education along with enjoyment. You will settle in one of the small adobe tasting rooms or in a shaded area outside.

The Mondavi tour guides share a word to the wise about wine tasting. "Just pretend you're eating a hamburger—look at it, smell it, and taste it. It's that simple."

During the tasting, questions and observations are encouraged. When a question is posed on the color of red wine related to vintage, the guide places a white linen napkin over a plate and pours a '79 Cabernet Reserve beside an '82 and an '87 to discuss the differences. Aging causes a slightly brown tinge due to oxidation, which shows on the napkin. Younger wines usually yield a more intense color.

With its vigorous dedication to the marriage of food with wine, the winery has a full complement of chefs who prepare meals for special events. At this writing, Mondavi is one of the few wineries that offer a taste of food other than crackers or bread to complement a tour's wine tasting. As an example, small squares of a peach tart—and its recipe—are offered in tandem with Moscato d'Oro dessert wine.

The educational tour and taste program was initiated at the opening of the Robert Mondavi Winery, at a time when there were only twenty-six active wineries in the Napa Valley. Since then, more than 180 wineries have grown along Highway 29 and the Silverado Trail as well as on western and eastern slopes. Through all the expansion, this winery has been a central beacon to visitors, growers, and vintners.

MUMM NAPA VALLEY

Mumm Napa Valley

8445 Silverado Trail
Rutherford, CA 94573
(707) 942-3434;
telefax (707) 942-3470

Winemaker: Greg Fowler
Winery owner: The Seagram
Classics Wine Company

Access

Location: 5 minutes' drive south of
St. Helena on the Silverado Trail,
between Highway 12 and Oakville
Cross Road.

Hours open for visits and tastings:
10:30 A.M.–6 P.M. daily. Tours on
the hour from 11 A.M.–4 P.M.

Appointment necessary for tour? No.

Wheelchairs accommodated? Yes.

Tastings

Charge for tasting with tour? $3.50
per flute (full glass); not deductible
from price of purchased wine.

Charge for tasting without tour?
As above.

Typical wines offered: Mumm
Cuvée Napa, Brut Prestige, Blanc de
Noir, Winery Lake Cuvée, and
limited releases available only at
the winery.

Sales of wine-related items?
Yes, including logo glass ($5).

Picnics and Programs

Picnic area open to the public? No.

Special events or wine-related
programs? Catered luncheons,
dinners, receptions, fine art
openings and permanent Ansel
Adams photography exhibit
entitled "The Story of a Winery."
Wine Club.

A California plantation house. While you sit on the veranda at Mumm Napa Valley, sipping sparkling Blanc de Noir and gazing westward over acres of Cabernet Sauvignon grapes, the image develops of a California-variety plantation. New-age flute music, white chairs, and creamy white Italian canvas umbrellas shading the sun's rays contrast with thriving green philodendron plants and verdigris metal chairs in the glass-enclosed exteriors of the hospitality center. Massive, Casablanca-style fans push soft breezes in the room while a young woman smiles and asks, "Sparkling wine or mineral water?"

This winery, which is one of the new establishments on the Silverado Trail, offers the California dream in contemporary style. Its facilities reveal the most modern wine-making equipment in the world.

Touring is easily done, all on one level, due to an excellent walkway system bordering the huge fermentation tanks. On autumn tours I have taken the tour guides have been articulate, aware of the stages of the wine-making art, and sophisticated enough to relate to visitors from a variety of backgrounds. In fact, in my opinion none of the tours and tour guides covered in this collection can rival Mumm Napa Valley, along with Robert Mondavi and St. Supéry, for comprehensive, visitor-friendly tours.

Your tour will depart from the visitors' center and proceed down a gravel path to a minivineyard where Pinot Meunier, Chardonnay, and Pinot Noir grapes grow. Since the fruit used for actual production is grown "down valley" in the Carneros region, the small vineyard is a practical demonstration of a year's cycle of grape growth. (The eighty acres of Cabernet Sauvignon vines surrounding the Mumm Napa Valley estate produce grapes to make Sterling wine. Sterling, Mumm Napa Valley, and Three Palms are all owned by the Seagram Classics Wine Company. G.H. Mumm et Cie of Reims, France, co-owns the Mumm Napa Valley venture.)

The tour guide is sure to mention that "Although all Champagne is sparkling wine, not all sparkling wines are Champagne." Almost every guide at every sparkling winery makes the same statement.

There is little discussion as you pass the fermentation tanks arranged as neatly as steel tanks in the most modern dairy. The largest tank of all is centrally located in the vast room. As its 65,000-gallon capacity is described in one-bottle measure, if you drank one 750-milliliter bottle of wine a day, it would take 898 years to empty the vat.

At the walkway's end, there is an observation platform from which you'll see the arrival area for grapes during harvest. If you visit this or any winery during "the crush," as grape harvest is called, you'll see action. Workers are laboring six, sometimes seven days a week, twelve to fourteen hours per day. The fruit is delivered in bins as yellow as mustard on a hot dog.

Greg Fowler, the winemaker who consults with French-trained Guy Devaux, has chosen the classic method of treating grapes for sparkling wines: The fruit is delivered to the winery in the same yellow box the grapes were picked in ("the famous yellow box") to ensure they arrive with skins undamaged. The boxes are then emptied directly into the press, with grapes still on the stem. Pressing with the stems creates space in the press, allowing the juice to flow more freely away from the skins. The skin contains both color and tannin (which has an astringent character undesirable in sparkling wine). The goal is to minimize their influence to the greatest degree possible. Only the first 72 percent of the juice pressed is used to produce Mumm Napa, with the remaining sold as bulk wine. "You want tannins in still wines," explains the tour guide, "but not in sparklers." When the just-crushed juice is siphoned into a tank, yeast is added immediately to help convert the juice's sugar into alcohol. This first fermentation method is identical to that of a still wine.

The difference in making sparkling wine in the *méthode champenoise* manner is that the wine is then funneled into heavy bottles, which are stopped with small plastic *bidules* (translates from French as "thingamajig"), which act as plugs. The bottles are then capped with a metal sodapop top. During the one-and-a-half to four years the bottles lie on their sides, ninety to a hundred pounds of pressure per square inch builds within each bottle. That's the same pressure as that of a car tire, applied to a wine bottle.

By now, you are in a wide corridor looking through windows at a variety of activities: to one side is the automatic riddling room where gyropallets are stacked with pallets of filled bottles. The gyropallets turn every six hours to encourage the sedimentary mass of dead yeast cells to collect at the bottle necks. On the other side of the corridor, you'll see the impeccable, large laboratory.

Look through yet another large window to view the freezing and disgorging treatments of the wine. Here, necks of bottles filled with aged, bottle-fermented wine are frozen automatically in a negative twenty-three degrees centigrade brine bath, followed by removal of the metal caps. This action forces the *bidules* and frozen plugs of yeast to burst from the bottles. The *dosage*—an addition of a small amount of sugar dissolved in wine—overcomes the tartness of the acidity and "softens" the wine.

Finally, on to a viewing station above the bottling line, where a hundred thousand cases of sparkling wine annually receive their corks, wire cages over the corks, labels, and neck foils. The whole procedure is fully automated and moves with the precision of a music box with dancing figures.

There is a wall-mounted demonstration of how champagne corks are made, with layers of glued cork pressed into a mass that is then cut. The tour guide will field questions with ease, and will act as your waiter on returning to the visitors' center. There, for a change, you can enjoy generous tastings of the various sparkling wines as well as sweet or savory appetizers while being shaded by Italian umbrellas and lulled by the strains of flute music.

California indeed.

Niebaum-Coppola Estate Winery

1991 St. Helena Highway
Rutherford, CA 94573
(707) 963-9099;
telefax (707) 963-9084

Winemaker: Scott McLeod
Winery owners:
Francis Ford and Eleanor Coppola

Access

Location: Highway 29, north of
Oakville in the town of Rutherford,
first left after Niebaum Lane.

Hours open for visits and tastings:
10 A.M.–5 P.M. daily except New
Year's Day, Easter, and Christmas.

Appointment necessary for tour?
Yes. Please call 963-9099 to
arrange tours.

Wheelchairs accommodated? Yes.

Tastings

Charge for tasting with tour?
$5 for five wines.

Charge for tasting without tour?
As above.

Typical wines offered: At least
one taste of Rubicon, one of the
Francis Coppola Family Wines and
one of the Gustave Niebaum
Commemorative Label vintages.

Sales of wine-related items? Yes.

Picnics and Programs
Picnic area open to the public? Yes,
around the fountain on upper hill.

Special events or wine-related
programs? Yes. Call the winery for
further information.

When you turn off Highway 29 onto the Rutherford property of the Niebaum-Coppola Estate Winery, imagine you're bouncing in a horse-drawn carriage down the one-fifth-mile entry drive. The earth to your right and left has yielded wine grapes since Finnish fur trader Captain Gustave Niebaum founded this winery in 1879. As you alight from your "carriage," you'll become aware of a deep sense of dual traditions here. Ivy-covered winery buildings face a square as large as the hub of some European towns. The original stone winery lies to the west of a massive reflecting pool. The ninety-foot-long pool was recently added as part of major interior and exterior refurbishing by Francis Ford and Eleanor Coppola, who are, since late 1994, the owners of this historic winery chateau in the heart of the Napa Valley.

The wine-making facility is a reminder of turn-of-the-century Bordeaux-style architecture. The particularly interesting mix here is the fact that renowned film director Coppola has put his stamp inside the stone building, with such additions as flashy *Dracula* costumes and furniture from the original set of *The Godfather*. The result? A mesh of old and new traditions, both bent on pleasing the public with memorable sights and wines.

For a beautiful view, walk the gentle slope to the crest of the hill just south of the chateau. There you will find the original fountain that was hauled by slow flatbed truck to its new home. It presides there over a panorama of vineyards, olive trees, and the Victorian home once the domicile of Captain Niebaum, now the private home of the Coppolas.

By noting the building's fine details, you will understand why it was five years in construction, opening in 1879. To best appreciate the place, step over the original "Inglenook" embedded in the stone entry and walk around the entry hall to view the Captain's Room. More a museum than a hospitality center, the room resembles a ship's ward room, down to its porthole window, shelf railings, and latched cupboard doors. The room and entry hall houses a 400-year-old glass lamp and sixteenth-century Flemish wine cups and other valuable items. From there you will face the grand staircase enhanced by buttery wooden pedestals hand-carved from wood imported from Belize (where the Coppolas own a lavish resort).

To the right is a series of rooms including a well-stocked retail space. Eleanor Coppola chooses the items, which range from *Apocalypse Now* T-shirts to pastas, home grown olive oil and a variety of stemware. Adjacent is the wine-tasting room and a unique multimedia room where you will taste wines while simultaneously watching a twelve-minute film on the Coppolas' dream. The winery pours numerous wine varietals, offering a chance to zero in on elegant vintages or wines for more relaxed dining.

Keep your eyes open as you walk about the chateau and you'll spy an original Tucker (featured in Coppola's film of the same name). Look to one side of the automobile and you'll see five Oscars amassed by the Coppolas over the years; turn again to find a glass-encased Niebaum and Inglenook memorabilia collection that evokes the inevitable sense of

living with history, once again demonstrating the two sides of tradition awaiting the winery visitor.

Another find is the extensive wine library to the left of the main entrance. The bottle collection houses Inglenook vintages back to 1887 and now shelves Niebaum-Coppola wines beside. Although ancient vintages are not available for public tasting, they are occasionally offered for extraordinary auctions or wine industry tastings.

During your stay at the winery, you will probably learn about the typical Napa Valley soil so important to the success of the wines. Ask any guide for information on the earth in this Rutherford region. You will find that it is rocky, well-drained, and alluvial. The first layer of soil typical in the Napa Valley, also called the top layer of "plowed pan," contains dark humus and the blue-gray Bale Clay, mixed together. History states that when Captain Niebaum bought the property, he diverted the stream to the north, but the underlying sandy and gravelly sediments from the meandering stream remain, yielding alluvial soil. Sandstone gravels and highly colored chert pebbles eroded from the third layer. Chert, changed as a result of high heat, proves past volcanic activity in the area. The fourth layer is an interface of cobbles incorporated with clay, and the base is bedrock. It is important to understand that poor, rocky soil requires roots to stretch and to hold it during their typically thirty-year lifespan.

An explanation of the soil sheds light on answers to two frequent questions concerning vineyard management:

How often do you water the vines? Rarely, if at all. Roots seek out the water level, which is twenty to thirty feet below the surface. However, vineyardists often install a drip irrigation system to handle overly dry soil during times of drought and extreme heat.

Do you uproot the vines frequently? There are some vines here in the Napa Valley that have survived well over fifty years. For example, Trefethen, Beringer, and Niebaum-Coppola are a few vineyards with rootstock of that age or older. The vines still bear fruit. In the Napa Valley, rootstock remains planted thirty years on average, unless there is a plant disease.

Real wine-making history was made by Captain Niebaum's great-nephew, John Daniel, Jr., during the thirty-year era he headed the company (1934 to 1964). Among other giant strides, Daniel promoted and gained acceptance for the Napa Valley appellation, pioneered vintage-dating of wines, and pushed for varietal designations for wines from the region, all steps toward solidifying the valley as a home of great wines.

What's upstairs in the chateau? Francis Coppola says that there will be a film museum in the near future. Other plans include a small cafe on the site, and a more prominent placement of the *Apocalypse Now* camouflage boat that presently rests in dry dock on the property. But these ideas are just the tip of Coppola's hopes for the future of the winery. Who knows what "Gustave's Godfather" will dream next?

JOSEPH PHELPS VINEYARDS

Joseph Phelps Vineyards

200 Taplin Road
St. Helena, CA 94574
(707) 963-2745;
telefax (707) 963-4831

Winemaker: Craig Williams

Winery owner: Joseph Phelps

Access

Location: On the Silverado Trail,
2 miles north of Zinfandel Lane,
turn onto Taplin Road—
it's the first winery on the left.

Hours open for visits and tastings:
9 A.M.–5 P.M., Monday–Saturday;
10 A.M.–4 P.M. Sunday. Scheduled
tours 1 P.M. and 2 P.M.

Appointment necessary for tours? No.

Wheelchairs accommodated? Yes.

Tastings

Charge for tasting with tour? $3.

Charge for tasting without tour?
As above.

Typical wines offered: Those
currently available—usually
four—including Cabernet
Sauvignon and Chardonnay.

Sales of wine-related items? Yes.

Picnics and Programs

Picnic area open to the public?
Yes, though not always available;
request permission in advance.

Special events or wine-related
programs? No

The forest green Spring Valley schoolhouse at Taplin Road along the Silverado Trail is a showstopper. The century-old school sits unchanged in a woodsy glen, marking the entrance to Joseph Phelps Vineyards property where you'll find one of the truly spectacular views in the valley, particularly at springtime. Drive up Taplin to the imposing gateway crafted from redwood bridge timbers. Once on Phelps's land, you may feel a sense of the Napa Valley as it was at the turn of the century. The reason for this hindsight vision is that Joe Phelps planted grape rootstock on only 175 acres of the former Connolly Hereford Ranch, thus maintaining rolling hills and erratic hillocks throughout 670 acres of prime land, much as when visits to neighboring ranches were by horse and buggy.

Phelps, who came to the valley with a background as a

contractor, is typical of those who visited and decided to remain. During the late 1960s, he was hired to build two Souverain wineries, then owned by the Pillsbury Company. Today those wineries are Rutherford Hill in the Napa Valley and Chateau Souverain in the Alexander Valley. As a result of those experiences, he purchased this property for his own winery, which he built in a big-timber, Colorado style. Massive redwood beams mesh with steel and glass, giving a feeling of solid new tradition built to last the test of time.

If you arrive in the spring, masses of pale violet wisteria will be draping the redwood timbers that bridge the winery's two pavilions—one housing the steel fermentation tanks and some small oak tanks, and the other housing the aging barrels made of French oak for Cabernets and Chardonnays and other wines, as well as Yugoslavian oak (used, because Yugoslavian oak does not impart flavors, for White Rieslings, Sauvignon Blancs, and Gewürztraminers). The wisteria hints at the beautiful flower beds awaiting the visitors, particularly those viewed while looking down the vineyard from the back patio.

Each time I've toured Phelps Vineyards, two distinct characteristics about the visitors have manifested themselves: first, many guests are true flower fanciers and come to view the plantings. Second, the tourists seem to be a fun-loving group. There is no explaining this latter enthusiastic spirit, unless it is the joie de vivre of the cheerful tour guides at the winery.

The tour commences on the patio in fair weather, or on the oriental carpet in the winery's foyer. There, visitors learn that this one winery produces twenty-five different varietal wines with a bottling of only a hundred thousand cases, a relatively small production for most wineries that have land holdings of four hundred acres (Phelps also owns vineyards in Oakville, Yountville, and Carneros).

Despite the quiet panorama from the patio, there is furious activity at the Taplin Road property. There actually are three active wineries here: besides the Phelps winery where all white wines are made, the winery's reds and its second label, Innisfree, are bottled in the property's former wine-making facility downhill. Third, Nyers Winery, owned by Phelps Vineyards president Bruce Nyers with backing from Joe Phelps, is also on the property.

For wine fanciers, there is much to learn here: Phelps exemplifies the use of stainless steel for fermentation, and it was at this winery that the true Syrah grape of France's Rhône Valley was first bottled in California, as opposed to the state's well-known Petit Sirah.

After visiting the 3,500 barrels in the cool fermentation chambers, a tasting under the patio arbor is perfectly timed. You'll taste at least six wines, perhaps more, depending on the tour guide and the time of day. Memorable touches include the cat, Georgette, who plays with guests, vying for attention as the tour guide speaks; and the shaded picnic area, which can be available but must be reserved ahead.

In fact, you could plan a complete Joseph Phelps-inspired outing: call ahead to reserve a tour and request a table at the Phelps picnic area, then shop at the Oakville Grocery on Highway 29 at Oakville Crossroad (the picnic-perfect grocery is one of Phelps's projects; it houses an array of cheeses, breads, wine, pastries, and international goodies). Once the basket is filled, head for "the Trail" and Taplin Road in time for your tour and then settle down for a relaxed outdoor meal with wine from the source. Such a day, wrapped in memories of wisteria and wine, will long be remembered.

Spelunkers, take notice: there are 36,000 square feet of caves in the eastern Napa Valley foothills above Rutherford Hill Winery. The cave system, which is 120 feet below ground in some areas, is the largest created for wine aging in North America. It was dug mechanically under the direction of Alf Bertleson during the 1980s and is secured with a gunnite surface.

So, what does an extensive cave system have to do with Rutherford Hill wine, or any wine, for that matter? The use of caves for wine storage is an ancient tradition. The French word for cellar is *cave*, and we English-speakers have adopted the word to mean a cavern or hollowed-out chamber of earth. Historically, wines have been aged in caves because the temperature within the earth is often as low or lower than the fifty to sixty degrees ideal for a slow, even fermentation of grape juice. Also, the humidity within caves is a constant 95 percent, reducing worry of wine evaporation through barrel pores. Caves have been used to store bottled wine as well, since the continuing fermentation in the bottle is deterred with cool storage.

For walking through the damp, labyrinthine caves, consider wearing rubber-soled shoes. With such a high humidity level, the cement floors, which are continuously hosed for sanitary purposes, tend to hold small pools of water, so sandals or high heels are bound to be uncomfortable. (A note on high heels in general for touring wineries: leave them in your car. They'll only slow you on gravel, in the fields, and in caves such as these.)

Rutherford Hill Winery grew from the successes of Freemark Abbey. In 1976, Freemark Abbey co-owners Chuck Carpy, Bill Jaeger, and Laurie Wood decided to expand their operation by purchasing the former Souverain of Rutherford winery, which had been built in the early seventies by Joseph Phelps. A later owner was Pillsbury Mills. By engaging a previously working, modern winery, the owners and winemaker Jerry Luper could immediately settle down to making wine from the thousand Napa Valley acres planted to grapes

on the owners' lands, with Merlot as their hallmark wine. This medium-sized winery produces 120,000 cases a year.

Driving to the winery, you'll journey up the hill that also leads to Auberge du Soleil, an elegant resort built Riviera-style along the hill's face. Both the resort and this winery at the crest overlook a picturesque view of the land grant given by pioneer George Yount to his granddaughter in the mid-1800s on the occasion of her marriage to Thomas Rutherford.

The forty-minute tour often opens with an invitation to picnic under the shady oaks in the Vaca Range, just above the winery or lower on the hill in an olive grove. A friendly, open spirit is maintained throughout the tour as you walk from the massive, barn-style hospitality center and winery up a slight incline to view the spectacular panorama, and then into the cave system. Barrels are stacked four barrels per pallet.

"Each barrel holds about sixty gallons of wine," notes the tour guide. "That's twenty-four cases per barrel." You can almost hear mental calculators whirring as tourists walk past cave after cave of neatly arranged French barrels. Interestingly, the barrels at Rutherford Hill arrive as precut staves, which are then assembled in Napa Valley by coopers at Demptos Cooperage. "We find it advantageous to construct and repair the barrels in our own backyard," the guide explains. The caves hold 7,250 barrels.

After touring a number of wineries, it becomes common-place to see bungs of varying construction. A bung is the closure for a wine barrel, and some are made of wood, some of plastic or silicone, some of glass, and yet others of earthenware. At Rutherford Hill, questions are frequently raised about paper cups used in place of more solid bungs, with the answer that those barrels are empty for the moment, awaiting washing or new wine.

If you are lucky enough to be led by a tour guide with a resonant voice, be prepared for a pleasant earful as the sound reverberates.

From the caves, the tour moves through the area of ninety stainless steel tanks, their dimpled encasements gleaming in the light. You will learn about various styles of filtration to clarify the wine for eventual bottling, including a high-tech Italian Velo filter and a state-of-the-art centrifuge.

Back at the visitors' center, you will be offered tastes of three wines. (This is one of the wineries that makes a point of offering free mineral water for designated drivers.) And if you are bound to shop, the retail outlet at Rutherford Hill offers items from wine chillers to posters to books on wine and food to a line of mustards, Napa Valley olive oil, and other foods.

Whether the fascination is with caves, wine making, or picnicking, Rutherford Hill can provide multiple diversions.

St. Clement Vineyards

2867 North St. Helena Highway
St. Helena, CA 94574
(707) 963-7221;
telefax (707) 963-9174

Winemaker: Dennis Johns
Winery owner: Sapporo USA

Access

Location: Just north of Deer Park Road on the southwest side of Highway 29.

Hours open for visits and tastings: 10 A.M.–4 P.M. daily except Easter, Thanksgiving, Christmas, and New Year's Day.

Appointment necessary for tour? Yes, with one to two hours notice.

Wheelchairs accommodated? Yes.

Tastings

Charge for tasting with tour? No.

Charge for tasting without tour? No.

Typical wines offered: All current releases of Sauvignon Blanc, Chardonnay, Merlot, Cabernet Sauvignon; often "library wines" as well.

Sales of wine-related items? Yes, including logo glasses ($5) and shirts.

Picnics and Programs

Picnic area open to the public? Yes, by appointment only.

Special events or wine-related programs? "Friends of St. Clement" are sent a newsletter and invited to attend an annual Christmas party and Harvest Festival. They are also notified of prereleases.

Immediately following harvest, leaves on the Chinese pistachio tree splash a vibrant red-orange circle of color along the south side of St. Clement Vineyards. This brilliant color contrasts dramatically with subtle gray-green wood siding and white trim on the Victorian home that crowns this western hillside vineyard just up the road from the Charles Krug Winery. Actually, the color of flames is symbolic of the phoenix existence this small gem of a winery has known since it was first built in 1876.

Fritz Rosenbaum, a San Francisco glass merchant who wished to join the estate vineyard boom in the Napa Valley, bought this property and constructed the tasteful home atop a small stone winery. The cellar was bonded in 1879, the eighth in the valley. Rosenbaum took great pride in producing his own wine, which he bottled under the name of Johanaberg Vineyards.

Then, during and after Prohibition, the winery fell into disrepair, until Michael Robbins, a real estate executive and wine connoisseur, bought the land in 1962 and renamed it

Spring Mountain Vineyards. Robbins took meticulous care in renovating the house, where he lived until he sold it to Dr. William Casey in 1975. At that point, Robbins moved to Tiburcio Parrot's Miravalle estate on Spring Mountain Road, taking with him the Spring Mountain Vineyards name and label.

Once again the elegant little Victorian on the hill took on a new name. Casey named it St. Clement Vineyards, after the small Chesapeake Bay home island of his Maryland family and also in honor of the patron saint of mariners.

Winemaker Chuck Ortman, who had made wines in the same cellars for Mike Robbins's Spring Mountain wines, created the early vintages of Chardonnay, Sauvignon Blanc, and Cabernet Sauvignon under the new label. Dennis Johns, formerly at Sterling Winery, is winemaker now, overseeing an annual production of ten thousand cases of wine, making this one of the smaller wineries in the valley.

The most recent metamorphosis for Fritz Rosenbaum's Victorian home and cellar took place in 1987 when the winery was purchased by Sapporo USA, a Japanese brewing and wine making company seeking to diversify its interests. This was the first Japanese group to invest in a Napa Valley winery, although the number has now increased to a half-dozen or more. Under the new proprietors, the winery home has finally opened its doors to the public, with daily tastings and tours.

Climb up the hill from the lower parking area, passing neatly manicured vineyards. The walk is steep, so enjoy the view as you go slowly. You'll stroll past an inviting porch swing and enter the living room-hospitality center where a tasting bar is arranged in a corner of the former dining room. The brief but informative tour departs from the tasting area, passes through the rooms on the first floor, and then moves on to the upper patio just beyond the front door. From there, you'll enjoy a splendid view across and down the valley no matter the season in which you're visiting.

The tour continues under the house in the barrel-lined stone cellar. The scent of fermenting grapes may hit you here more than in larger wineries because of the relatively small dimensions of this space. Wine having been aged in the cellar since the 1880s, that aroma has permeated even the stone and timbers supporting the house.

Out into the daylight and up a gentle hill, you'll come to a

newer stone building that houses the fermenting tanks. Most probably you will meet the winemaker, who is open to answering queries about techniques, cold stabilization, the harvest, or whatever is on your mind. The tour guides are extremely friendly, acting more like aunts and uncles welcoming visiting relatives than group leaders. The groups here tend to mirror the winery's small size—you will probably share the visit with six or fewer travelers. After visiting the fermentation area, a return to the tasting room completes the walking tour and a generous tasting ensues.

There is little wonder why St. Clement's charm has captured many TV commercial producers and is frequently mistaken for a bed and breakfast inn. It stands solitary on its hill, a reminder of the gracious way of life here a century ago.

**St. Supéry Vineyards
and Winery**

8440 St. Helena Highway
Rutherford, CA 94573
(707) 963-4507;
telefax (707) 963-4526
800-942-0809

Winemaker: Michael Schulz
Winery owner: Skalli Corporation

Access

Location: On Highway 29 midway
between the towns of Oakville and
Rutherford, on the northeast side
of the highway.

Hours open for visits and tastings:
9:30 A.M.–4:30 P.M. daily, except
Christmas and New Year's Day.
Tours given continuously.

Appointment necessary for tour? No.

Wheelchairs accommodated? Yes.

Tastings

Charge for tasting with tour?
$2.50; not deductible from price
of purchased wine.

Charge for tasting without tour?
As above.

Typical wines offered: All current
releases of Sauvignon Blanc,
Chardonnay, Cabernet Sauvignon,
Moscato, and Merlot.

Sales of wine-related items? Yes,
including logo glasses ($3.95).

Picnics and Programs
Picnic area open to the public?
Yes, with permission of visitor
center staff.

Special events or wine-related
programs? Art shows and chamber
music concerts.

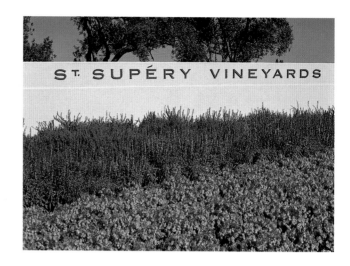

Wedding gifts at the turn of the last century were occasionally offered in land, rather than lace tablecloths or family photos in silver frames. In fact, this fifty-six-acre winery in the midst of George C. Yount's original five-hundred-acre Rancho Caymus land grant was the dowry gift for Bartlett Vine's marriage to Ellen Yount. She was a daughter of George C. Yount, the prominent landowner who first planted grape-stock in the Napa Valley. Later, in 1881, brothers Joseph and Louis Atkinson bought the land and built a home near the hundred-year-old oak tree that shaded a corner of the vine-yard. When winemaker Edward St. Supéry lived in the house, from 1904 to 1920, his home was a magnet for winemakers of the day—Charles Krug, Jacob Beringer, and Jacob Schram were frequent visitors.

A strong sense of history accompanies a visit to St. Supéry, despite the fact that the winery is one of the more recently established estates along Highway 29. Perhaps it is the juxta-position of the new and the old: the state-of-the-art straight lines of the wine production area contrast with the lush lawn and floral landscaping fronting the Queen Anne Victorian Atkinson house. Or perhaps it is the gracious, old-fashioned hospitality with which tourists are greeted. Among its several lures, the St. Supéry Winery has appeal for all ages and wine-appreciation levels.

St. Supéry, named after French winemaker Edward St. Supéry, offers guided tours as well as unescorted tours. Especially if you arrive during harvest, don't miss the guided tour. It winds from the lobby of the modern winery out through the Atkinson house (which is open for tours only and is decorated with authentic 1880 furnishings appropriate for a summer home) and past a gazebo into the exhibition vineyard. There, visitors are encouraged to pick varieties of grapes grown for St. Supéry wines. Of all the winery tours in this collection, only this winery offers you the chance to pick as many grapes as you wish—the closest approximation to "working the crush," which is an unspoken but frequent dream of August and September visitors to the Napa Valley.

While in the vineyard, the tour guide discusses the Dollarhide Ranch, the winery's vineyard of fifteen hundred acres in Pope Valley, northeast of St. Helena. The size alone puts St. Supéry among the ten largest vineyards for land holdings, despite the fact that the new winery is now operating at only a small percentage of its production capacity.

From the vineyard, the tour returns to the production side of the operation. With a 536,000-gallon tank capacity and the ability to bottle 2,500 cases per day, it is clear that Robert Skalli of France, owner of St. Supéry, has plans for major wine production in the future. Already there are 150 employees at the winery.

As the tour continues on a wide catwalk over massive stainless steel tanks, the well-trained guide points out icy build-up on some of the tank walls, due to cold stabilization of white and red wines. When the temperature is dropped well below normal, any sediment in the wine will drop to the bottom of the tank and be easily removed, eliminating visible tartrates. Another plus of a harvest tour here is the outdoor viewing platform directly above the hopper where grapes are received and sent to the crusher-stemmer.

The rest of the tour is a guided version of the self-guided option offered during the winery's open hours. Locals call the St. Supéry self-guided tour "touchy-feely," although the clearly defined walk in the air-conditioned, carpeted space is primarily geared to the senses of sight and smell. For instance, there is a wooden model of a vineyard that is surrounded on four sides with descriptions of the operations of a vineyard year. (See page 21.) Anyone who previously thought that growing wine grapes was a simple pastime will quickly reconsider.

"Sniffers" are favorite learning devices on the walk-around tour. Here, tourists can smell aromatic essences to help identify certain characteristics in wine. By using a special display, guests smell cedar, bell pepper, cherry, and black pepper related to red wine aromas. White wine "whiffs" are grapefruit, green olive, dried wildflower, and new-mown hay.

Moving from aromas to wine tasting is a natural step, one that is rewarded with samples of at least five wines: Sauvignon Blanc, Chardonnay, Cabernet Sauvignon, Atkinson House Red, and the delicate Moscato. The latter two are available only at the winery. The well-appointed shop offers wines, T-shirts, books on the region, and items related to wine and food.

Culture is very important to the directors of St. Supéry. Be sure to view the changing art shows on display in the entry and tasting areas. And, if you are in the valley for a few days, ask whether the winery is presenting any cultural events, such as a chamber music concert.

SCHRAMSBERG VINEYARDS

Schramsberg
Vineyards

1400 Schramsberg Road
Calistoga, CA 94515
(707) 942-4558;
telefax (707) 942-5943

Winemaker: Mike Reynolds
Winery owners:
Jack and Jamie Davies

Access

Location: 5 miles north of
St. Helena on Highway 29,
turn southwest onto Peterson
and make a quick right onto
Schramsberg Road.

Hours open for visits and tastings:
By appointments and for tours only,
seven days a week, 10 A.M.,
11:30 A.M., 1 P.M., 2:30 P.M.
(subject to change). No tours
Fourth of July, Labor Day,
Thanksgiving, and Christmas.

Appointment necessary for tour?
Yes; the day before, if possible.

Wheelchairs accommodated? Yes.

Tastings
Charge for tasting with tour?
$6.50, not deductible from cost of
purchased wine.

Charge for tasting without tour?
Tastings offered with tour only.

Typical wines offered: Blanc Blanc,
Blanc Noir, Brut Rosé, Cremant,
Reserve, and J. Schram.

Sales of wine-related items? Yes.

Picnics and Programs
Picnic area open to the public? No.

Special events or wine-related
programs? No.

The Schramsberg hillside winery and caves epitomize the romance of wine making in the Napa Valley. Very little has changed on the exterior of this estate since it was founded in 1862 by Jacob and Annie Schram, emigrés from Germany. In fact, Jack and Jamie Davies, who have owned the winery since 1965, refuse to widen the seven-tenths-mile Schramsberg Drive from Highway 29 to their property because that change would disturb the natural beauty and the tradition of the drive up the hill. As a result, the county grants a limited tasting permit, and this is one of the few Napa Valley wineries that offers wine samples with tours only.

The lack of samples does not dissuade thousands of visitors who travel here every year to encounter the source of Schramsberg's celebrated Napa Valley *méthode champenoise* (aged in the bottle) sparkling wines. The tourists come with the same interest in wine and lifestyle that beckoned the Davies to the wine country, when they left the Southern California corporate life.

"We call it Napa Valley Champagne," explains Jamie Davies, "because French Champagne is perceived as the finest of that country's sparkling wine. We didn't want to hint at lesser quality here."

The Davies live in Jacob Schram's original Victorian home with a wide veranda overlooking cascading flowers and the entry to the caves. The home was built in the 1880s, coinciding with winery construction at Beringer, Chateau Montelena, Inglenook, and estates now known as St. Clement and Spring Mountain.

From the 1860s through the turn of the last century, wineries flourished in the Napa Valley, with more than eighteen thousand acres planted to vines by 1900. It was during that early heyday of the local wine industry that Robert Louis Stevenson frequently visited Jacob Schram. Later he devoted a chapter to the Schramsberg estate in his "Silverado Squatters." (For further information on the famous writer, visit the Robert Louis Stevenson Museum in the town of St. Helena.)

During Prohibition and with a variety of owners, the winery rested. Its hand-dug underground cellar system remained in disrepair until 1965, when the Davies came across the Schram Estate after an extensive search for a winery property. They purchased the neglected estate and set about planting Chardonnay, Pinot Noir, and Pinot Blanc vines, to which they have since added a Californian grape: Flora.

The tour begins at the upper crush pad area near the parking lot, below the private home. You will pass fragrant plantings of rosemary and other herbs, as well as mulberry trees and palm trees. Most Napa Valley palm trees were planted at the turn of the century; they were considered exotic status symbols. As you drive the valley's length, note the placement of palms like tufted elephants' legs in the bright Napa sun. Many have been growing a century or more.

Below the house, an amusing bronze statue of a rakish frog, Champagne flute in hand, seems to rise out of the lotus pond fronting the entrance to the caves. Once inside the visitors' center, you'll see numerous photos of VIPs in the worlds of politics, art, and music, all related to menus of dinners where Schramsberg has been served since its first Blanc de Blanc release in 1969.

The cellars are well lit, with rows of poker-table-green light fixtures illuminating the walls of Champagne bottles. At least two million bottles rest on their sides, with a hundred pounds of pressure in each bottle. The bottles remain dormant until the winemaker decides the proper time for riddling, the turning action that moves the dead yeasts down to the neck of each bottle.

"We house up to six years of vintages of the reserves here," points out the tour guide, "and that's only one of our five styles of Napa Valley Champagne."

Of all the caves in this valley, those at Schramsberg come closest to the ambiance of the catacombs of Paris and other such dank, romantic subterranean cellars. Moss clings to the walls and water oozes from the rocky mountainside.

If you're seeking a hands-on experience, do try the riddling exercise in the caves. Watching master riddler Ramon Biera give rows of Champagne bottles a one-sixth turn makes the symmetrical action seem effortless—until you try it. "Fingers only! Don't use your wrist!" cheerleads the tour guide as visitors volunteer to try their hand—rather, their fingers—at the art. And Ramon's fifteen years of riddling forty thousand to sixty thousand bottles daily suddenly make him a hero.

"What happens if a bottle drops?" asks a tourist. He learns that Champagne bottles are much heavier than standard wine bottles to counteract the fermenting pressure; however, a Champagne bottle would shatter into thousands of shards if dropped on cement.

Exiting the cave feels like departing from the Tunnel of Love. From corridors of darkness into daylight, you walk to the mechanized arena of wine making: riddling machines there turn five hundred bottles of Blanc de Blanc, reducing the manual work time for those bottles by half. (The other four styles of Schramsberg Champagne are hand-riddled.)

Even while you stay behind the yellow line, you will be quite close to the disgorging, corking, and labeling lines in the final stage of this tour. Thirty percent of the pressure and 10 percent of the wine is lost with the disgorging action. You'll hear a dull "thunk, thunk, thunk" as the bottles' metal caps are removed and the frozen plug of sediment flies out of the bottle. Then a small *dosage* of sugar or brandy or cognac is added to sweeten the sparkling wine, followed by immediate corking and labeling.

After seeing the various stages a bottle must endure in this process of making sparkling wine, one tourist remarked that she would never again complain about the cost of a bottle of Napa Valley Champagne.

STAG'S LEAP WINE CELLARS

Stag's Leap Wine Cellars

5766 Silverado Trail
Napa, CA 94558
(707) 944-2020;
telefax (707) 257-7501

Winemaker: Warren Winiarski
Winery owners:
Warren and Barbara Winiarski

Access
Location: From Napa, take Trancas
Street to the Silverado Trail;
the winery is 7 miles north on the
east side.

Hours open for visits and tastings:
10 A.M.–4:30 P.M. daily, except
Easter, Thanksgiving, Christmas,
and New Year's Day.

Appointment necessary for tour? Yes.

Wheelchairs accommodated? Yes.

Tastings
Charge for tasting with tour? $2,
including logo glass; not deductible
from cost of purchased wine.

Charge for tasting without tour?
As above.

Typical wines offered: Current
releases of Cabernet Sauvignon,
Chardonnay, Sauvignon Blanc,
and White Riesling.

Sales of wine-related items? Yes.

Picnics and Programs
Picnic area open to the public?
Yes. Request permission from staff.

Special events or wine-related
programs? The *Stag's Leap Wine
Cellars News* notifies those on
the mailing list of a yearly open
house and seminars offered
throughout the year.

There is a sense of serious dedication to integrity and fine wine making imparted during a visit to Warren and Barbara Winiarski's Stag's Leap Wine Cellars. Since 1970, the former University of Chicago political science lecturer has insisted on stressing his vines and tightening the space between rows of Cabernet Sauvignon vines, so the roots will stretch as deep as thirty feet in soil he rarely irrigates. This soil lies on the south end of the Stags Leap District, which runs along the Silverado Trail from Clos du Val (just south of Stag's Leap Wine Cellars) to the Oakville Cross Road. To the workers at the winery as well as the Winiarskis, that soil and the grapes harvested annually from the vines are the source of happiness and success.

It was Stag's Leap Wine Cellars' 1973 Cabernet Sauvignon that took highest honors during the pivotal Paris blind tasting in May 1976, when a Napa Valley Chardonnay (Chateau Montelena) and this Cabernet changed the global sea of opinion and earned waves of adulation for California wine. The truly amazing fact is that Winiarski's grapes had been plucked from three-year-old vines, usually considered too immature to produce complex flavor. "That winning gave us the foothold we have today," mentions tour guide Marilyn Landeros.

As you would expect, a man who takes his wines so seriously mirrors his philosophy in tours at this winery. The basic tour here runs about a half-hour; however, Stag's Leap Wine Cellars draws true wine connoisseurs as visitors and their questions often demand detailed explanation. Count on an hour if you are scheduling the day.

You will walk under ancient oak trees based with profuse plantings of ornamental strawberries and wild roses. In summer, the bouquet from the flowers can be overpowering. You will move past the roof-covered fermentation tanks and on to the original crush pad. Occasionally Barbara Winiarski will greet guests and answer a few questions.

"You know, we never imagined we'd need a second phone, much less a second building," she commented about the physical growth of the winery since its 1971 opening. "That's why the five structures on the property have such basic names: Building 1, Building 2, and so on." There is little room here donated to frivolous extras, but tourists will experience an active small winery with a mom-and-pop feel.

Tour guides are extremely well-informed and cover such topics as irrigation systems, acidity, Brix levels, the effects of drought, and the mix of clay, volcanic soil, and pebbles that creates ideal soil conditions for growing Cabernet Sauvignon grapes. You will pass through the indoor-outdoor fermentation area and then walk uphill to the French oak barrel aging building.

Workers in knee-high rubber boots continue their winery work, moving hoses, climbing the pyramids of barrels to "top off" any air space, and hosing the cement floors to maintain the impeccable conditions necessary to wine.

Discussion will continue about grape types, malolactic

fermentation, growers, and microclimates. For some tourists, this visit will include more than they want to know; for others, this will be winery tour heaven.

The tour concludes at the long wooden table in Building 2 where various vintages are poured, including Hawk Crest, the winery's second label. The tasting moves in standard pattern: first the white wines, followed by the heavier, more tannic red wines. Mineral water is available for designated drivers. By the time of tasting, the small, disparate group of visitors has had a chance to meet and there is a sense of camaraderie, with an occasional exchange of addresses.

The shady picnic area on the face of the winery property just above the parking area offers tables and chairs in a garden setting. This can be a quiet rest stop for motorists and bicyclists as well—all that is needed is "a loaf of bread and thou." The bottle of wine is readily at hand.

Note: There is some confusion concerning punctuation for clarity in the names Stag's Leap Wine Cellars and Stags' Leap Winery and the appellation Stags Leap District. The Stags Leap District appellation was designated officially in the late eighties and is spelled without apostrophe. Carl Duomani's Stags' Leap Winery connotes a number of stags, whereas Winiarski's wine refers to a single stag.

Sterling Vineyards

1111 Dunaweal Lane
Calistoga, CA 94515
(707) 942-3344;
telefax (707) 942-3467

Winemaker: Bill Dyer
Winery owner: The Seagram
Classics Wine Company

Access

Location: 1 mile south of Calistoga off Dunaweal Lane, between Highway 29 and the Silverado Trail.

Hours open for visits and tastings: 10:30 A.M.–4:30 P.M. daily, except Thanksgiving, Christmas, and New Year's. Continuous tours.

Appointment necessary for tour? No.

Wheelchairs accommodated? Tasting room and parts of tour.

Tastings

Charge for tasting with tour? $6, includes sky tram ride to winery, tour, sit-down tasting, and picnic access; $2 visitor discount from first bottle of wine purchased.

Charge for tasting without tour? No tasting without tour.

Typical wines offered : Current releases of Chardonnay, Sauvignon Blanc, Merlot, Cabernet Sauvignon, Pinot Noir, and more. Limited private cellar wine—additional fee.

Sales of wine-related items? Yes, including logo glass ($5).

Picnics and Programs

Picnic area open to the public? Yes.

Special events or wine-related programs? The Seagram's School of Service and Hospitality offers 25 consumer courses yearly; also, a winter luncheon series. The New Release Club and Special Selection Club offer prerelease notice and discounts and invitations to special events.

The panoramic vista from the bell-tower deck at Sterling Vineyards is one of the most spectacular in the Napa Valley. From there you will see mountain ranges encircling the valley floor, with a sweep broad enough to include Highway 29 and the Silverado Trail in one glance. During the spring, rust-colored farmsteads and bright blue reservoirs contrast with a central carpet of yellow mustard flowers blooming at the base of dormant rootstock vines. And in the Mediterranean style of this winery, olive trees and cypresses frame the extensive property.

When the winery was built, in 1973, the idea was to create a place of prominence by placing the winery's pure white arches, towers, and castlelike walls high above the valley floor. At the same time, architect Martin Waterfield constructed a cool mountainside area for the chai (barrel aging area) by building it vertically into the hill and lighting it through gemlike stained glass windows.

Because of the labyrinthine driving paths and the narrow roads to the top of the estate, a sky tram (five dollars per person) was devised to transport visitors over gardens, vineyards, and a small lake, to the arrival dock, where a self-guided tour begins. Follow the informational placards to learn about wine making in the grand style. Sterling, which is owned by the Seagram Classics Wine Company, produces eleven varietal wines here from grapes grown on its 1,100 acres of Napa Valley vines, and has a fermentation capacity of almost five hundred thousand gallons. The signs will direct you from station to station and, even on a busy day, you'll rarely have the sense of being in a crowd.

There is quite a bit of walking up and down stairs on this visit, including a steep climb to the final tasting room stop. On a blisteringly hot day, take it slowly.

Once in the tasting room area, you can relax in the spacious air-conditioned interior or you may choose to sit on the outdoor patio. From the terraces, you'll look through pines, redwoods, and some oaks up-valley toward Calistoga. Clos Pegase winery is in view, as are occasional gliders from the Calistoga airport nearby.

While in the visitors' center, you'll learn of The Seagram Classics School of Service and Hospitality, which offers classes primarily for members of the restaurant and wine industry. There is also St. Dunstan's dining room, decorated in medieval style and available for private dinners.

By the time of descent via tram to the parking lot, you will have learned a considerable amount about wine making and you'll have been to the top of the world in the middle of the valley.

Sutter Home Winery

277 St. Helena Highway
Helena, CA 94574
(707) 963-3104;
telefax (707) 963-2381

Winemaker: Gary Brenham
Director of Winemaking:
Steve Bertolucci
Winery owner: The Trinchero family

Access

Location: 1 mile south of St. Helena
on the southwest side of Highway
29, at the large white Victorian.

Hours open for visits and tastings:
Retail open 9 A.M.–5 P.M.; tasting
room open 10 A.M.–4:30 P.M.,
except Easter, Thanksgiving,
Christmas, and New Year's Day.
Winery tours given continuously.

Appointment necessary for tour?
No. Self-guided garden tours.

Wheelchairs accommodated?
In tasting room, not in gardens.

Tastings

Charge for tasting with tour? No.

Charge for tasting without tour? No.

Typical wines offered: Current
releases of White Zinfandel,
Sauvignon Blanc, Chardonnay,
Chenin Blanc, Zinfandel, Reserve
Zinfandel, Cabernet Sauvignon,
Merlot, and Gewürztraminer.

Sales of wine-related items?
Yes, including four logo glasses
(prices vary, $2.95–$5.95).

Picnics and Programs
Picnic area open to the public? No.

Special events or wine-related
programs? The *Sutter Home
Newsletter* is a quarterly featuring
new releases and recipes.

If an easy self-tour is your goal in visiting a winery, Sutter Home is an ideal destination. The visit to this winery, known largely for its White Zinfandel, consists of walking around the perimeter of a large room with a central wine tasting bar.

The room's space is divided into individual dioramas depicting scenes from a turn-of-the-century home. Examples of wall and floor coverings are painted in appropriate places, and some of the furnishings are of that period. For instance, the parlor includes comfortable period armchairs and a fireplace with old-time portraits framed and on the mantelpiece. Signs of life punctuate the scene: a basket with knitting here, a book there. And each diorama includes a description of how that part of the home—the porch, the kitchen, the conservatory, and the windowsill—fit into the daily life of the American family.

You may overhear older tourists waxing nostalgic when they see a treasure that reminds them of their youth. On the other hand, younger members of a touring party might identify with the Victorian dollhouse and other toys on display or learn about former home necessities no longer a part of our modern life.

Tiles line the walkway inside the winery's visitors' center. There is no treatment of vineyards and grapes here, with the exception of a display of old wine production machines, some photos of wine-making procedures, and a placard that presents the story of the winery. Wine is described as an enhancement to daily life in the style of the good old days.

Among such depictions of yesteryear, the nostalgia level is high. But the natural is also celebrated, in the present-day garden just outside the visitors' center, which is alive with eight hundred varieties of flowers, trees, and plants in the beds surrounding the 1884 Victorian home on the property. Garden tours are available and well worth the walk. You'll see beds of exquisite roses, scented geraniums, free-form wisteria, butterfly bushes, and trees such as weeping flowering cherry and Japanese maple. If photographing flowers is a hobby for you, be sure to visit Sutter Home midsummer for the best color and floral varieties.

Although the home is closed to the public, tourists are encouraged to rest in the garden gazebo and relax, remembering a time when life was slower.

The Trinchero family, which now owns Sutter Home, traces the winery's history back to 1890, when it was the first wooden winery in the valley. "The story of Sutter Home is a slice of Americana," reads the notice at the interior entry to the tasting room. "Its fate rose and fell with impacts of World Wars I and II, with Prohibition, the Depression, the Great Immigration of Europeans to the United States and the San Francisco earthquake and fire of 1906. That year, Sutter Home, every acre, every building, was sold for $10 gold."

Today's Sutter Home, which rose to success on the wings of White Zinfandel's popularity in the 1970s and 1980s, is now one of the most profitable wineries in the country. Its actual (and huge) wine production area is a few miles away, off Zinfandel Lane, where nearly four million cases of wine are produced annually from Napa Valley and other California grapes. But the winery center on Highway 29 just south of St. Helena continues to draw thousands of tourists who yearn to trace the roots of their favorite wine—"White Zin."

SUTTER HOME WINERY
EXECUTIVE OFFICES
NOT OPEN TO THE PUBLIC

Please Visit Our
Tasting Room Next Door

Trefethen Vineyards

1160 Oak Knoll Avenue
Napa, CA 94588
(707) 255-7700;
telefax (707) 255-0793

Winemaker: David Whitehouse, Jr.
Winery owners:
The Trefethen family

Access

Location: 2 miles north of the town of Napa, take Oak Knoll Avenue to the Trefethen entrance.

Hours open for visits and tastings: 10 A.M.–4:30 P.M. daily except New Year's Day, Easter, Thanksgiving, and Christmas; Tours given at 10:30 A.M. and 2:30 P.M.

Appointment necessary for tour? Yes, 24 hours in advance.

Wheelchairs accommodated? Limited.

Tastings

Charge for tasting with tour? $4, deductible from price of purchased wine.

Charge for tasting without tour? $4, which includes glass.

Typical wines offered: Current releases of Chardonnay, Cabernet Sauvignon, White Riesling.

Sales of wine-related items? Yes, including books, logo glasses, and shirts.

Picnics and Programs

Picnic area open to the public? No.

Special events or wine-related programs? No.

The Trefethen family has a deep pride in its six hundred contiguous acres of vineyards, the largest plot under single ownership within the Napa Valley. As a result, tourists quickly learn the history of the land and how it relates to the winery estate.

The drive onto the property from Oak Knoll Avenue can be reached easily from the Silverado Trail or Highway 29. As you enter, signs mark clearly the various grape varieties—Pinot Noir, Chardonnay, Cabernet Sauvignon. The old winery dominates the property with its massive form, painted the Tuscan orange of a winter sunset. White and pink oleanders fringe the winery, and gnarled oaks cast shadows on the walls.

Founded in 1886, the former Eshcol winery was the earliest three-story gravity-flow winery in the county. It produced wine until 1940, with a hiatus during Prohibition (1920–1933), during which time the government granted permission for making sacramental or personal-use wines only.

Vestiges of earlier days are evident in the visitors' entry room where the tour begins. You'll see photos of the land when it was planted to walnut and prune orchards and as it was in 1968 when Gene and Katie Trefethen chose this land with the dream of remodeling the Eshcol winery and planting grapes once again. Trefethen was living a corporate dream of the 1970s—he was then president of Kaiser Industries—and it was time to settle down and make wine.

"We are a destination winery," declares a guide to a small group of tourists. "Fifty percent of our visitors already know Trefethen wines and are willing to drive here to find us"; he adds, "and we prefer people who are interested in wine." There is the advantage in an intimate-size group that you can stop at any point and ask questions, which are encouraged and are answered in depth.

This is a "backwards" tour, in the sense that the first areas you'll visit—the barrel aging rooms—are not first in the sequence of wine making. But since Trefethen was a gravity-flow winery originally it makes sense to see barrels where they used to rest over a hundred years ago.

In a gravity-flow winery, grapes are crushed, stemmed, and fermented on the top floor. The fermented juice is next aged in barrels on the second floor, then moved to the ground level for bottling and shipping.

The stairs to the second floor of the winery are narrow. You'll view a majority of small oak barrels, which hold enough wine to fill 325,000 750-milliliter bottles. Note the silicone bungs in the barrels. These barrel stoppers are made of an inert material that provides a tighter seal than the standard wooden bungs. "Compared to serious loss in the past due to air seepage, only two barrels a year are affected now," explains the tour guide.

Wherever you tour Napa Valley wineries, you will hear discussion of the "toast" of the oak in various wines. Trefethen Vineyards makes the effort to discriminate the various stages of toastiness: there is a display of woods from six different oak barrel interiors, each of which has been carefully charred to develop a certain level of toasted oak flavor. Later, during wine tasting, the guide will point out the "toast" quality of the various wines.

Moving from the main building, the tour passes the crush pad and crusher-stemmer. During harvest, you are in clear view of grape delivery and all the swift stages that take place from arrival of the grapes in open-topped gondolas (fruit-bearing trailers) to the fermentation stage. In the modern spirit of this winery, 60 percent of all harvesting takes place mechanically, usually in the evening or early morning when the grapes are cool and their skins are firm enough not to be damaged by the picking action.

The fermentation tanks, bottling line, and other stages of production are quite accessible. "Everything you see," points out the guide, "from vine to bottle, is done on our land. Therefore, it can be called 'estate bottled'—all our wines are estate bottled."

Wending the way back to the old winery, you may pass the small plot of seventy-five-year-old Zinfandel vines that the Trefethen family keeps, unpruned, as a reminder of earlier times. Taste the grapes, if it is harvest time—the fruit has a brawny sweetness. And just imagine the history of those vines, which have stood time's test through vintages of happiness and hardship.

V. SATTUI WINERY

V. Sattui Winery

1111 White Lane
St. Helena, CA 94574
(707) 963-7774;
telefax (707) 963-4324

Winemaker: Rick Rosenbrand
Winery owner: Darryl Sattui

Access

Location: On Highway 29, ½ mile
south of St. Helena, across from
the Beacon Service Station.

Hours open for visits and tastings:
9 A.M.–6 P.M. daily, March through
October; 9 A.M.–5 P.M., November
through February, except Christmas
Day. Self-guided tours.

Appointment necessary for tour?
Not for self-guided tours; required
for private tours and groups.

Wheelchairs accommodated? Yes.

Tastings

Charge for tasting with tour? Not
with self-guided tour; private or
group tour/tasting charge is $75
per group or $2.50 per person,
whichever is greater. Not deductible
from price of purchased wine.

Charge for tasting without tour? No.

Typical wines offered: Current
releases of at least eight wines,
featuring Sauvignon Blanc, and
Johannisberg Riesling. Also, estate
Gamay Rouge, Zinfandel, and
Cabernet Sauvignon.

Sales of wine-related items?
Yes, including logo glasses.

Picnics and Programs

Picnic area open to the public? Yes.
Special events or wine-related
programs? The Wine of the Month
program (in the U.S.). Cellar Club
offers six annual events: two
Harvest Balls, Crush Party, Barrel
Tasting Party, Tax Relief Party, and
Dixieland Jazz Festival in July.

Cheese and picnics, picnics and cheese. Napa Valley tourists' first impressions about the V. Sattui Winery just south of St. Helena relate to picnics, due to the two acres of shaded tables and benches fronting Highway 29. Beds of flowers, ancient oak trees, and a wine tasting room and delicatessen enhance the visual invitation to turn off the road and relax.

Since the Napa Valley weather is relatively clement, about 250,000 visitors take advantage of the picnic area year-round. An Italian-style stone building dominates the land, with multilevel terraces, porches, and fountains decorating the front of the building.

This winery (built in 1976, although it appears older) is a far cry from Vittorio Sattui's Bryant Avenue Winery in San Francisco's North Beach. That company produced wine from 1885 to 1921 and then closed due to Prohibition. It was not until Vittorio's grandson, Daryl Sattui, reestablished the winery and moved it to St. Helena that the family name was again affiliated with wine.

The tour at V. Sattui is an extremely relaxed self-tour. As you walk the property and visit the various levels of the winery, you'll find signs describing the history of the ancient artifacts arranged outdoors, such as antique carts that used to transport wine in barrels. You are free to roam, to picnic, and to shop in the large retail store that offers breads, cheeses, wine, and wine-related items. In fact, V. Sattui is one of the largest distributors of imported cheese in Northern California.

The emphasis here is shy when it comes to wine making, with the exception of wine promotion in the retail shop. There is a barrel-lined underground stone wine cellar where weddings, private tastings, and meetings take place; otherwise, the importance is placed on those redwood tables out front.

The winery produces thirty thousand cases annually and keeps its overhead low by selling all its wine through the tasting room, along with cheese and picnics, picnics and cheese.

Resources

Note: All Resources are in the 707 Telephone Area Code

Chambers of Commerce

Calistoga Chamber of Commerce
1458 Lincoln Avenue, Calistoga
942-6333

Napa Chamber of Commerce
1556 First Street, Napa
226-7455

St. Helena Chamber of Commerce
1010 Main Street, St. Helena
963-4456

Yountville Chamber of Commerce
6795 Washington Street, Yountville
944-0904

Educational Sources

The Culinary Institute of America
Greystone Cellars
2555 Main Street, St. Helena
963-4503

Meadowood Wine School
Meadowood Resort
900 Meadowood Lane, St. Helena
963-3646

Napa Valley College
Napa-Vallejo Highway, Napa
253-3000

School for American Chefs
Beringer Vineyards
2000 Main Street, St. Helena
963-7115

Seagram Classics School of Service and Hospitality
Post Office Box 365, Calistoga
942-0832

Libraries

Calistoga Library
1108 Myrtle Street, Calistoga
942-4833

Napa County Library
580 Coombs Street, Napa
253-4241 or 800-248-8402

Napa Valley Wine Library
1492 Library Lane, St. Helena
(within St. Helena Library)
963-5145

St. Helena Library
1492 Library Lane, St. Helena
963-5244

Yountville Library
6548 Yount Street, Yountville
944-1888

Museums

Bale Grist Mill
California State Park System
On Highway 29 between St. Helena and Calistoga, on west side of the road
963-2236

Calistoga City Museum
1311 Washington Street, Calistoga
942-5911

The Hess Collection
4411 Redwood Road, Napa
255-1144

Napa County Museum
473 Main Street, St. Helena
(in Vintage Hall)
963-7411

Robert Louis Stevenson Museum
Silverado Museum
1490 Library Lane, St. Helena
963-3757

Sharpsteen Museum
1311 Washington Street, Calistoga
942-5911

Newspapers

The Weekly Calistogan
1360 Lincoln Avenue, Calistoga
942-6242

Napa Register
1615 Second Street, Napa
226-3711

St. Helena Star
1328 Main Street, St. Helena
963-2731

Magazines

Appellation
1040 Main Street, Napa
255-2525

TOURING AND WINE MAKING

ON TOURING WINERIES

Touring these and all other Napa Valley wineries is gratis. Occasionally there is a charge for the wines tasted or for a wine glass bearing the winery's logo.

Like restaurants, many wineries prefer to know their guest count, for obvious reasons. Although phone numbers are rarely taken when you book a tour, it is polite to call in to cancel. A tour guide may be brought in just for your party, particularly at the smaller wineries.

It is ideal to arrive at least five minutes before a tour, leaving time to locate and join the tour group.

In most cases, it is acceptable to arrive just before a tour and join in, but at wineries that request reservations politeness suggests calling ahead, even that same morning.

Stay with the group, remembering that these are working wineries.

Expect noise from tractors, bottling machines, fork lift machines, and other equipment. In other words, be prepared for action.

On attire: casual clothing is the norm. After all, you'll be visiting working areas that often include newly turned earth or moist floors. Even on a blisteringly hot day, you may wish to bring a light wrap for touring the caves and wineries. They are air-conditioned to around fifty-five degrees, whether by nature or machines, and the contrast in temperature is noticeable.

Some people collect etched wine glasses from the various wineries that sell such stemware.

Small wineries are willing to talk of distributors in specific areas; large wineries don't need to. But if you wish to know how to find a certain wine in your home town, do not hesitate to ask the tour guide.

It's not necessary to drink all the wine offered during a tasting. Use the dump buckets or spit buckets that are placed on the tasting bars for that purpose.

During any tour, expect a variety of levels of wine knowledgeability among the visitors. Don't be shy about asking questions.

On footware: it's a good idea to wear rubber-soled shoes. Since the winery business must be as sanitary as the dairy business, cleanliness is extremely important. Therefore, the floors of the winery are frequently wet from hosings. Also, closed-toe shoes are recommended for visiting wineries that include in-vineyard tours.

Tour guides are often excellent sources for restaurant recommendations.

It is illegal to serve wine to minors, which includes anyone under the age of twenty-one.

There is no smoking in cellars or tasting rooms.

You are encouraged to take photographs.

ON WINE AND WINE MAKING

Wine is fermented grape juice.

There is only one harvest annually, in the autumn.

The local name for harvest is "the crush."

The vintage year on a bottle relates to the year the grapes were picked.

Wine derives its natural sugar from the fruit itself; it is illegal to add sugar to wines made in California.

Grapes do not like "wet feet." There is little, and often no, irrigation in the miles of vineyards. The grape rootstock has long roots, which seek the natural water level as deep as thirty feet underground.

Every state in the nation, except Alaska, grows grapes to make wine.

California grows over 75 percent of the country's wine grapes, 90 percent of the table grapes, and all of the raisin grapes.

The Napa Valley holds approximately 31,000 acres of land planted to vineyards, which is only 6 percent of the state's wine grapes.

To store wine while driving in the valley, keep it upright within the car (presuming you have not opened the bottle). Do not store it in the trunk, particularly during extreme heat; the trunk will act as an oven and actually cook the wine.

One plastic lug full of grapes holds forty pounds of fruit.

Sparkling wine is popularly served in stemware called a flute. The flat coupe-shaped Champagne glasses popular in the past were said to have been based on the form of Marie Antoinette's left breast.

Notice the shapes of still wine bottles. Those with "sloping shoulders" are based on techniques used originally in the Burgundy region of France. Those with "square shoulders" are based on wines of the Bordeaux region. Historically, the early reason for shouldering wine bottles was for tax purposes: the tax collector could define the source of the wine easier by "reading the shoulders."

Wine is the only alcoholic beverage that improves with aging after bottling and corking.

September first is often the date for prices for the newly released wines.

Check with your tour guide about shipping wine home. In most cases, it is illegal to ship from the winery; however, there are local wine shops that can handle the transport process for you.

These are the graduated sizes of wine bottles:

Tenth . . . . 375 milliliters
Standard . . . . 50 milliliters
Jeroboam . . . . 4 standard bottles, 3.0 liters
Rehoboam. . . . . 6 standard bottles, 4.5 liters
Methuselah. . . . . 8 standard bottles, 6.0 liters
Salmanazar. . . . . 12 standard bottles, 9.0 liters
Balthazar. . . . . 16 standard bottles, 12.0 liters
Nebuchadnezzar. . . . . 20 standard bottles, 15.0 liters

On Barrels

Wine aging barrels, cut in half, are often available, for example for use as planters or table bases. Ask your tour guide whether the winery has any for sale or where they could be found nearby.

A "barrel tasting" refers to tasting wine directly out of the aging barrel. (It has nothing to do with tasting the barrel itself!)

A full barrel weighs 490 pounds.

New French barrels cost around $600.

New American barrels cost around $250.

One French barrel holds sixty gallons, the equivalent of twenty-five cases of wine.

Each case of wine holds nine liters of beverage.

American oak barrels are made in Tennessee.

French barrels have full, broad "bellies" with wide space between steel bands at the center; American barrels are more uniformly shaped, with steel bands at relatively even widths across the barrel.

Barrels are often stacked on wooden triangular wedges. Also, you will see them on wooden pallets, steel squared-off frames, and on wooden frames.

If red-wine barrels seem old and stained compared to pristine white-wine barrels, your observation is correct. Grape juice for red wines is colored by steeping it on the grape skins. The resultant red color stains barrels and gives them an appearance of age.

A Directory of Napa Valley Wineries

Note: All wineries are in the 707 Telephone Area Code

ACACIA WINERY
2750 Las Amigas Road
Napa 94559
226-9991

AETNA SPRINGS CELLARS
7227 Pope Valley Road
Pope Valley 94567
965-2675

ALTAMURA WINERY
4240 Silverado Trail
Napa 94558
253-2000

AMIZETTA VINEYARDS
1099 Greenfield Road
St. Helena 94574
963-1053

S. ANDERSON VINEYARDS
1473 Yountville Crossroad
Yountville 94599
944-8642

ANDERSON CONN VALLEY
680 Rossi Road
St. Helena 94574
963-8600

ARROYO WINERY
2361 Greenwood Road
Calistoga 94515
942-6995

DAVID ARTHUR VINEYARDS
1519 Sage Canyon Road
St. Helena 94574
963-5190

ARTISAN WINES
5335 Redwood Road
Napa 94558
252-6666

ATLAS PEAK VINEYARDS
3700 Soda Canyon Road
Napa 94581-0660
252-7971

BARNETT VINEYARDS
4070 Spring Mountain Road
St. Helena 94574
963-0802

BEAUCANON
1695 St. Helena Highway
St. Helena 94574
967-3520

BEAULIEU VINEYARDS
1960 St. Helena Highway
Rutherford 94573
963-2411

BENESSERE VINEYARDS
1010 Big Tree Road
St. Helena 94574
963-5853

BERGFELD WINERY
401 St. Helena Highway South
St. Helena 94574
963-7293

BERINGER VINEYARDS
2000 Main Street
St. Helena 94574
963-7115

BOUCHAINE VINEYARDS
1075 Buchli Station Road
Napa 94558
252-9065

BUEHLER VINEYARDS
820 Greenfield Road
St. Helena 94574
963-2155

BURGESS CELLARS
1108 Deer Park Road
St. Helena 94574
963-4766

CAIN CELLARS
3800 Langtry Road
St. Helena 94574
963-1616

CAKEBREAD CELLARS
8300 St. Helena Highway
Rutherford 94573
963-5221

CALAFIA CELLARS
4411 Redwood Road
Napa 94558
963-0114

CAPORALE WINERY
910-H Enterprise Way
Napa 94558
253-9230

CARNEROS ALAMBIC
DISTILLERY
1250 Cuttings Wharf Road
Napa 94559
253-9055

CARNEROS CREEK WINERY
1285 Dealy Lane
Napa 94558
253-9463

CASA NUESTRA
3451 Silverado Trail
St. Helena 94574
963-5783

CAYMUS VINEYARDS
8700 Conn Creek Road
Rutherford 94573
963-4204

CHANTER WINERY
2411 Third Avenue
Napa 94558
252-7362

CHAPPELLET VINEYARD
1581 Sage Canyon Road
St. Helena 94574
963-7136

CHATEAU BOSWELL
3468 Silverado Trail
St. Helena 94574
963-0351

CHATEAU CHEVALIER
3101 Spring Mountain Road
St. Helena 94574
963-2342

CHATEAU CHEVRE WINERY
2030 Hoffman Lane
Yountville 94599
944-2184

CHATEAU MONTELENA
1429 Tubbs Lane
Calistoga 94515
942-5105

CHATEAU POTELLE
3875 Mount Veeder Road
Napa 94558
255-9440

CHATEAU WOLTNER
150 White Cottage Road South
Angwin 94508
965-2445

CHIMNEY ROCK WINERY
5550 Silverado Trail
Napa 94558
257-2641

CLOS DU VAL
5330 Silverado Trail
Napa 94558
259-2200

CLOS PEGASE
1060 Dunaweal Lane
Calistoga 94515
942-4981

CODORNIU NAPA
1345 Henry Road
Napa 94558
224-1668

CONN CREEK WINERY
8711 Silverado Trail
St. Helena 94574
963-5133

CONN VALLEY VINEYARDS
680 Rossi Road
St. Helena 94574
963-8600

LOUIS CORTHAY WINERY
996 Galleron Road
St. Helena 94574
963-2384

COSENTINO WINERY
7415 St. Helena Highway
Yountville 94599
944-1220

COSTELLO VINEYARDS
1200 Orchard Avenue
Napa 94558
252-8483

CUVAISON WINERY
4550 Silverado Trail
Calistoga 94515
942-6266

DALLA VALLE VINEYARDS
7776 Silverado Trail
Napa 94558
944-2676

DEER PARK WINERY
1000 Deer Park Road
Deer Park 94576
963-5411

DeMOOR WINERY
7481 St. Helena Highway
Oakville 94562
944-2565

DIAMOND CREEK VINEYARDS
1500 Diamond Mountain Road
Calistoga 94515
942-6926

DOMAINE CARNEROS
1240 Duhig Road
Napa 94559
257-0101

DOMAINE CHANDON
1 California Drive
Yountville 94599
944-2280

DOMAINE MONTREAUX
4101 Big Ranch Road
Napa 94558
252-9380

DOMAINE NAPA WINERY
1155 Mee Lane
St. Helena 94574
963-1666

DUCKHORN VINEYARDS
3027 Silverado Trail
St. Helena 94574
963-7108

DUNN VINEYARDS
805 White Cottage Road
Angwin 94508
965-3642

EL MOLINO
P.O. Box 306
St. Helena 94574
963-3632

EVENSEN VINEYARDS
WINERY
8254 Highway 29
Oakville 94562
944-2396

FAR NIENTE WINERY
1 Acacia Drive
Oakville 94562
944-2861

FLORA SPRINGS WINERY
1978 West Zinfandel Lane
St. Helena 94574
963-5711

FOLIE À DEUX
3070 St. Helena Highway
St. Helena 94574
963-1160

FORMAN VINEYARDS
1501 Big Rock Road
St. Helena 94574
963-0234

FRANCISCAN OAKVILLE
ESTATE
1178 Galleron Road
Rutherford 94573
963-7111

FREEMARK ABBEY WINERY
3022 St. Helena Highway
St. Helena 94574
963-9694

FRISINGER CELLARS
2277 Dry Creek Road
Napa 94558
255-3749

FROG'S LEAP WINERY
8815 Conn Creek Road
Rutherford 94573
963-4704

GIRARD WINERY
7717 Silverado Trail
Oakville 94562
944-8577

GOOSECROSS CELLARS
1119 State Lane
Yountville 94599
944-1986

GRACE FAMILY VINEYARD
1210 Rockland Road
St. Helena 94574
963-0808, (800) 227-5152

GRAESER WINERY
255 Petrified Forest Road
Calistoga 94515
942-4437

GREEN AND RED VINEYARD
3208 Chiles Pope Valley Road
St. Helena 94574
965-2346

GRGICH HILLS CELLARS
1829 St. Helena Highway
Rutherford 94573
963-2784

GROTH VINEYARDS
750 Oakville Crossroad
Oakville 94562
944-0290

HAGAFEN CELLARS
P.O. Box 3035
Napa 94558
252-0781

HARRISON VINEYARDS
1527 Sage Canyon Road
St. Helena 94574
963-8726

HAVENS WINE CELLARS
1441 Calistoga Avenue
Napa 94558
255-7337

HEITZ WINE CELLARS
436 St. Helena Highway
St. Helena 94574
963-3542

THE HESS COLLECTION
WINERY
4411 Redwood Road
Napa 94558
255-1144

WILLIAM HILL WINERY
1761 Atlas Peak Road
Napa 94558
224-6565

HONIG CELLARS
850 Rutherford Road
Rutherford 94573
963-5618

JAEGER INGLEWOOD
CELLARS
2125 Inglewood Avenue
St. Helena 94574
963-1875

JOHNSON TURNBULL
8210 St. Helena Highway
Oakville 94562
963-5839

JUDD'S HILL
P.O. Box 415
St. Helena 94574
963-9093

KATE'S VINEYARD
5211 Big Ranch Road
Napa 94558
255-2644

ROBERT KEENAN WINERY
3660 Spring Mountain Road
St. Helena 94574
963-9177

HANNS KORNELL
CHAMPAGNE CELLARS
1091 Larkmead Lane
St. Helena 94574
963-1237

CHARLES KRUG WINERY
2800 Main Street
St. Helena 94574
967-2201

LA JOTA VINEYARD
1102 Las Posadas Road
Angwin 94508
965-2878

LA VALLETTE WINERY
2915 Soda Canyon Road
Napa 94558
252-2570

LA VIEILLE MONTAGNE
3851 Spring Mountain Road
St. Helena 94574
963-9059

LAKESPRING WINERY
2055 Hoffman Lane
Napa 94558
944-2475

LAMBORN FAMILY
VINEYARDS
2075 Summit Lake Drive
Angwin 94508
(415) 547-4643

LIMUR
771 Sage Canyon Road
St. Helena 94574
963-3726

LIVINGSTON WINES
1895 Cabernet Lane
St. Helena 94574
963-2120

LONG VINEYARDS
1535 Sage Canyon Road
St. Helena 94574
963-2496

LUNA VINEYARDS
2921 Silverado Trail
Napa 94558
255-5862

MACAULEY VINEYARD
3291 St. Helena Highway North
St. Helena 94574
963-1123

MALLARD WINERY
4162 Big Ranch Road
Napa 94558
255-4583

MARCH'S MOUNTAIN
3000 Summit Drive
Angwin 94508
965-9173

MARKHAM VINEYARDS
2812 North St. Helena Highway
St. Helena 94574
963-5292

LOUIS M. MARTINI WINERY
254 South St. Helena Highway
St. Helena 94574
963-2736

MATERA WINE CELLARS
4340 Silverado Trail North
Calistoga 94515
942-6283

MAYACAMAS VINEYARDS
1155 Lokoya Road
Napa 94558
224-4030

MEADOWROCK WINERY
3148 Soda Canyon Road
Napa 94558
224-4788

MERLION WINERY
880 Vallejo Street
Napa 94559
226-5568

MERRYVALE VINEYARDS
1000 Main Street
St. Helena 94574
963-2225

METZGER VINEYARD
PIGS LEAP
3243 St. Helena Highway North
St. Helena 94574
963-0711

MILAT VINEYARDS WINERY
1091 South St. Helena Winery
St. Helena 94574
963-0758

ROBERT MONDAVI WINERY
7801 St. Helena Highway
Oakville 94562
(800) MONDAVI,
or 226-1395 locally

MONT ST. JOHN CELLARS
5400 Old Sonoma Road
Napa 94559
255-8864

MONTICELLO CELLARS
4242 Big Ranch Road
Napa 94558
253-2802

MOSS CREEK WINERY
6015 Steele Canyon Road
Napa 94558
252-1295

MT. VEEDER WINERY
1999 Mount Veeder Road
Napa 94558
224-4039

MUMM NAPA VALLEY
8445 Silverado Trail
Rutherford 94573
942-3434

NAPA CREEK WINERY
1001 Silverado Trail
St. Helena 94574
963-9456

NEWLAN VINEYARDS
5225 Solano Avenue
Napa 94558
257-2399

NEWTON VINEYARD
2555 Madrona Avenue
St. Helena 94574
963-9000

NEYERS WINERY
1226 Conn Valley Road
St. Helena 94574

NICHELINI WINERY
2970 Sage Canyon Road
St. Helena 94574
963-0717

NIEBAUM-COPPOLA
ESTATE WINERY
1991 St. Helena Highway
Rutherford 94573
963-9099

OPUS ONE
P.O. Box 6
St. Helena Highway
Oakville 94562
963-1979

PAHLMEYER WINERY
P.O. Box 2410
Napa 94558
255-2321

ROBERT PECOTA WINERY
3299 Bennett Lane
Calistoga 94515
942-6625

PEJU PROVENCE WINERY
8466 St. Helena Highway
Rutherford 94573
963-3600

ROBERT PEPI WINERY
7585 St. Helena Highway
Oakville 94562
944-2807

MARIO PERELLI-MINETTI
WINERY
1443 Silverado Trail
St. Helena 94574
963-8762

JOSEPH PHELPS VINEYARDS
200 Taplin Road
St. Helena 94574
963-2745

PINA CELLARS
8060 Silverado Trail
Rutherford 94573
944-2229

PINE RIDGE WINERY
5901 Silverado Trail
Napa 94558
253-7500

PLAM VINEYARDS
6200 Washington Street
Yountville 94599
944-1102

POPE VALLEY WINERY
6613 Pope Valley Road
Pope Valley 94567
965-9463

BERNARD PRADEL CELLARS
2100 Hoffman Lane
Yountville 94599
944-8720

PRAGER WINERY AND
PORTWORKS
1281 Lewelling Lane
St. Helena 94574
963-3720

QUAIL RIDGE WINERY
1055 Atlas Peak Road
Napa 94558
257-1712

KENT RASMUSSEN WINERY
2125 Cuttings Wharf Road
Napa 94559
252-4224

RAYMOND VINEYARDS
849 Zinfandel Lane
St. Helena 94574
963-3141

REVERE VINEYARD
AND WINERY
2456 Third Avenue
Napa 94558
224-7620

RITCHIE CREEK VINEYARD
4024 Spring Mountain Road
St. Helena 94574
963-4661

ROMBAUER VINEYARDS
3522 Silverado Trail
St. Helena 94574
963-5170

ROUND HILL WINERY
1680 Silverado Trail
Rutherford 94574
963-5251

RUSTRIDGE VINEYARD
AND WINERY
2910 Lower Chiles Valley Road
St. Helena 94574
965-2871

RUTHERFORD HILL WINERY
200 Rutherford Hill Road
Rutherford 94573
963-7194

RUTHERFORD VINTNERS
1673 St. Helena Highway
Rutherford 94573
963-4117

SADDLEBACK CELLARS
7802 Money Road
Oakville 94562
963-4982

ST. CLEMENT VINEYARDS
2867 North St. Helena Highway
St. Helena 94574
963-7221

ST. SUPÉRY VINEYARDS
AND WINERY
8440 St. Helena Highway
Rutherford 94573
963-4507

SAINTSBURY
1500 Los Carneros Avenue
Napa 94599
252-0592

SAN PIETRO VARA VINEYARDS
AND WINERY
1171 Tubbs Lane
Calistoga 94515
942-5733

SCHRAMSBERG VINEYARDS
1400 Schramsberg Road
Calistoga 94515
942-4558

SCREAMING EAGLE WINERY
7557 Silverado Trail
Napa 94558

SEAVEY VINEYARDS
1310 Conn Valley Road
St. Helena 94574
963-8993

SEQUOIA GROVE VINEYARDS
8338 St. Helena Highway
Rutherford 94573
944-2946

SHADOW BROOK WINERY
360 Zinfandel Lane
St. Helena 94574
963-2000

SHAFER VINEYARDS
6154 Silverado Trail
Napa 94558
944-2877

CHARLES F. SHAW VINEYARD
AND WINERY
1010 Big Tree Road
St. Helena 94574
963-5459

SIGNORELLO VINEYARDS
4500 Silverado Trail
Napa 94558
255-5990

SILVER OAK CELLARS
915 Oakville Crossroad
Oakville 94562
944-8808

SILVERADO HILL CELLARS
3103 Silverado Trail
Napa 94558
253-9306

SILVERADO VINEYARDS
6121 Silverado Trail
Napa 94558
257-1770

ROBERT SINSKEY VINEYARDS
6320 Silverado Trail
Napa 94558
944-9090

SKY VINEYARDS
1500 Lokoya Drive
Napa 94558
935-1391

SMITH-MADRONE VINEYARDS
4022 Spring Mountain Road
St. Helena 94574
963-2283

SPOTTSWOODE WINERY
1401 Hudson Avenue
St. Helena 94574
963-0134

SPRING MOUNTAIN
VINEYARDS
2805 Spring Mountain Road
St. Helena 94574
963-5233

STAGLIN FAMILY VINEYARDS
P.O. Box 321
Rutherford 94573
963-1749

STAG'S LEAP WINE CELLARS
5766 Silverado Trail
Napa 94558
944-2020

STAGS' LEAP WINERY
6150 Silverado Trail
Napa 94558
944-1303

STAR HILL WINERY
1075 Shadybrook Lane
Napa 94558
255-1957

STELTZNER VINEYARDS
5998 Silverado Trail
Napa 94558
252-7272

STERLING VINEYARDS
1111 Dunaweal Lane
Calistoga 94515
942-3344

STONEGATE WINERY
1183 Dunaweal Lane
Calistoga 94515
942-6500

STONY HILL VINEYARD
P.O. Box 308
St. Helena 94574
963-2636

STORYBOOK MOUNTAIN
3835 Highway 128
Calistoga 94515
942-5310

STREBLOW VINEYARDS
2849 Spring Mountain Road
St. Helena 94574
963-5892

SULLIVAN VINEYARDS
1090 Galleron Lane
Rutherford 94573
963-9646

SUMMIT LAKE VINEYARDS
2000 Summit Lake Drive
Angwin 94508
965-2488

SUTTER HOME WINERY
277 St. Helena Highway
St. Helena 94574
963-3104

SWANSON VINEYARDS
AND WINERY
1271 Manley Lane
Rutherford 94573
944-1642

PHILIP TOGNI VINEYARD
3780 Spring Mountain Road
St. Helena 94574
963-3731

TRAULSEN VINEYARDS
2250 St. Helena Highway
Calistoga 94515
942-0283

TREFETHEN VINEYARDS
1160 Oak Knoll Avenue
Napa 94558
255-7700

TRUCHARD VINEYARDS
3234 Old Sonoma Road
Napa 94559
253-7153

TUDAL WINERY
1015 Big Tree Road
St. Helena 94574
963-3947

TULOCAY WINERY
1426 Coombsville Road
Napa 94559
255-4064

TURNBULL WINE CELLARS
8210 St. Helena Highway
Oakville 94562
963-5839

V. SATTUI WINERY
1111 White Lane
St. Helena 94574
963-7774

VAN DER HEYDEN VINEYARD
4057 Silverado Trail
Napa 94558
257-0130

VIADER VINEYARDS, INC.
1120 Deer Park Road
St. Helena 94574
963-3816

VICHON WINERY
1595 Oakville Grade
Oakville 94562
944-2811

VILLA ENCINAL
620 Oakville Crossroad
Oakville 94562
945-1220

VILLA HELENA WINERY
1455 Inglewood Avenue
St. Helena 94574
963-4334

VILLA MT. EDEN
8711 Silverado Trail
St. Helena 94574
963-5133

WERMUTH WINERY
3942 Silverado Trail
Calistoga 94515
942-5924

WHITEHALL LANE WINERY
1563 St. Helena Highway
St. Helena 94574
963-9454

WHITFORD CELLARS
4047 East Third Avenue
Napa 94558
257-7065

YVERDON VINEYARDS
3787 Spring Mountain Road
St. Helena 94574
963-5188

ZD WINES
8383 Silverado Trail
Napa 94558
963-5188

INDEX

Ahern, Albert, 60

Aiken, Joel, 30

barrels, 62–63, 73, 87, 111

Barrett, James P.
    and James L., 36

Barthman, Kent, 86

Beaulieu Vineyards, 30

Beringer, Jacob, 37, 90

Beringer Vineyards, 32–33

Bertolucci, Steve, 98

Biever, Margrit, 73

bottle sizes, 111

Brenham, Gary, 98

Cakebread Cellars, 34–35

canopy management, 56–57

Carpy, Charles, 60, 86

Casey, Michael, 38

Casey, William, 88

caves, 24, 86

Champagne Taittinger, 50

Chandon Club, 54

Chateau Montelena, 36–37

Chimney Rock Winery, 38–39

Clos du Val, 40–41

Clos Pegase, 42

Codorniu Napa, 44–45

cold stabilization, 40–41

Coppola, Francis Ford
    and Eleanor, 78

Crane, Eileen, 50

Cuvaison Winery, 48–49

Davies, Jack and Jamie, 92

Deis, Kenneth, 56

DeLatour, Georges, 30

Delgadillo, Ignacio, 60

Devaux, Guy, 76

Dollarhide Ranch, 90

Domaine Carneros, 50–51

Domaine Chandon, 54–55

Dyer, Bill, 96

Dyer, Dawnine, 54

Edwards, Ted, 60

Esser, Manfred, 48

estate-bottled, 101

Ewer, Seneca, 30

Fletcher, Douglas, 38

Flora Springs Winery, 56–57

Fowler, Greg, 76

Frank, Yort and Jeanne, 36

Freemark Abbey Winery, 60

Garvey family, 56

Goelet, John, 40–41

"Grapes of Laugh," 42

Graves, Michael, 42

Grgich Hills, 62–63

Grgich, Miljenko, 62

Hess Collection Winery, 64

Hess, Donald, 64

Hills, Austin, 62

Innisfree, 82

Jaeger, Bill, 86

Johns, Dennis, 88

Johnson, Randle, 64

Kamman, Madeleine, 32

Komes, Jerome and Flora, 56

Krug Winery, 68–69

Lichine, Alex, 39

Luper, Jerry, 86

Martini, Louis M., 56

Martini, Michael, 70

Martini Winery, 70

Maudière, Edmund, 54

McLeod, Scott, 78

Moët-Hennessey–
    Louis Vuitton, 54

Mondavi, Cesare, 69

Mondavi, Peter, 68–69

Mondavi, Tim, 72

Mondavi Winery, 72–73

Moynier, John, 68

Mumm Napa Valley, 76–77

Napa Valley: history of, 14;
    land use in, 15;
    soil of, 78

Niebaum, Gustave, 78–79

Nyers Winery, 82

organic farming, 57

Ortman, Chuck, 88

Pagano, Janet, 44

Phelps, Joseph, 82

Phelps Vineyards, 82–84

phylloxera, 57

picnics, 25

Portet, Bernard, 40–41

Quinones, John, 42

Rennie, William
    and James, 56

Reynolds, Mike, 92

Rhine House, 32–33

Robbins, Michael, 88

Robinson, Kevin, 86

Rosenbaum, Fritz, 88

Rosenbrand, Rick, 102

Rutherford Hill Winery, 86–87

St. Clement Vineyards, 88–89

St. Supéry Vineyards
    and Winery, 90–91

Sattui, Darryl, 102

Sbragia, Ed, 32

Schmidheiny, Alexander, 48

School for American Chefs, 52

Schramsberg Vineyards, 92–93

Schulz, Michael, 90

Searle, Ronald, 40–41

Sharpsteen Museum, 60

Shrem, Jan and Mitsuko, 42

Skalli, Robert, 90

sparkling wine, 25, 55, 76

Spring MountainVineyards, 88

Stag's Leap Wine Cellars,
    94–95

Sterling Vineyards, 96

Sutter Home Winery, 98

Tchelistcheff, André, 30

Thatcher, John, 48

Trefethen Vineyards, 100–101

Triay, Domingo, 44

Trinchero family, 98

Tubbs, Alfred, 36

Tychson, Josephine, 60

V. Sattui Winery, 102

vineyards: annual cycle in, 21;
    management of, 79

Waterfield, Martin, 96

Whitehouse, David, Jr., 100

Williams, Craig, 82

Wilson, Sheldon and Stella, 38

Wine: making, 110–11;
    transporting, 37

wineries: directory of, 114–17;
    by region and town, 24;
    selection of, 16–17;
    for special interests, 24–25;
    tours of, 26, 110;
    visiting seasons for, 24

wine thief, 38

Winiarski, Warren
    and Barbara, 94

Wood, Laurie, 60, 86

Yount, George, 54, 87, 90